Faith and Addiction

J B MYERS

FAITH AND ADDICTION

A FAITH ALTERNATIVE TO THE TWELVE STEPS THEORY AND DISEASE MODEL OF ADDICTION TREATMENT

2007

Faith and Addiction

TABLE OF CONTENTS

ACKNOWLEDGEMENTS

I owe a debt of gratitude to many for their help with this book. This effort reflects the knowledge and encouragement I have gained from many sources. I thank my family, which includes my wife, Jeanette, my sons, Jason, Joey, and Jared, and my mother, Myrl C. Myers. They have all positively affected my life and given me insight and wisdom. Betsy Gilliland has helped me to proof the manuscript for errors. LuNell Gilliland suggested some changes in style that have greatly improved the readability of the book. I thank Jane Hawkins and Clyde Slimp for providing me with feedback on the content of this book. I also thank Dr. Patricia Markos and others in the counseling department at the University of Nevada, Las Vegas for the training I received in counseling and addiction studies. And finally, I thank Tiny Malone for help with the front cover.

DEDICATION

This book is dedicated in memory and honor of my friend and mentor, Boyd Gilliland (1931-2005). Boyd is like Nathanael in the New Testament, of whom Jesus said, "Here is a true Israelite, in whom there is nothing false" (John 1:47).

INTRODUCTION

The purpose of this book is to give religious people an alternative to the Twelve Steps theory, Alcoholics Anonymous (AA), and the disease model of addiction treatment. Religious people who use biblical teaching as a guide for their lives are the primary focus of attention, but even those who have no religious faith can benefit from the issues covered in this book.

The argument of this book is that religion and faith work best in stopping addiction when it is accompanied by a cognitive, choice approach to behavior. Today, religious people tend to be either neglected or misdirected to deterministic approaches like Twelve Steps and the disease model of addiction. It is hoped that this book can offer an alternative that is both biblically based and more effective than what is currently presented to religious people.

This book is designed to be used as a resource for those who wish to explore the relationship of faith, spirituality, and addiction. Discussion questions at the end of each chapter are designed to help the reader process the information in the chapter and encourage further discussion. Recommendations for further reading in this book provide resources for those who would like more information on chapter topics. I do not claim to have all the answers to addiction treatment and I humbly invite those with greater knowledge in this area to offer suggestions for improvement and further discussion.

All quotations from Scripture are from the New International Version (NIV) of the Bible.

All stories and illustrations in this book are true, but names have been changed to protect privacy. To further protect privacy, some stories are composites.

Chapter 1
Drugs and Addiction

Melba's Story

Nicotine addiction is a choice, but it is not an easy choice. The story of Melba illustrates the faulty thinking and self-deception that often accompanies this and other addictions. Melba was addicted to nicotine and she refused to stop. Some would argue in her defense that her addiction was so bad that she was physically unable to stop, but this is, however, one of the great myths of addiction. Addiction is not the result of involuntary behavior, but of choices we make about our behavior. These choices are based on our values as well as the lies we tell ourselves about what we are doing.

Over the years, Melba's health began to deteriorate. Her heart, circulation, diabetes, and breathing problems were either caused or exacerbated by smoking cigarettes. Her family, friends, and doctors all urged her to stop smoking for the sake of her health, but Melba's favorite response was, "At least, I'll die happy!" One day she visited the doctor about circulation problems in her legs. The doctor told her these problems were negatively impacted by her smoking and that she should stop immediately. Her response was, "Doctor, I can't quit, but at least, I'll die happy." The doctor replied, "Melba, I hate to tell you this, but you are not going to die happy. I am afraid we are going to have to cut off your legs. It may already be too late, but if you will stop smoking, I will work with you to try and save your legs." Melba never smoked another cigarette, and she followed a health plan that allowed her to keep her legs for the rest of her life. Although Melba thought she was helpless in her addiction, she stopped smoking when faced with the choice of losing her legs or smoking cigarettes.

Another myth that drug addicts love to believe is summed up in the famous saying, "Eat, drink, and be merry, for tomorrow we shall die." The problem with this saying is that most addicts do not die the next day. Instead, they live long enough to experience all of the negative consequences their addictions bring them. I have counseled with people who have spent most of their adult lives either in prison or homeless because of their drug habits. As a result, they are now in middle age and suddenly realize they are not prepared for retirement. For the most part, they have no job skills, and because they have not worked regularly, they do not even have social security. Because of their addictions, they have ruined their health, destroyed relationships, and consigned themselves to a lifetime of poverty. They are basically alone and without any resources.

What can be done for those who sacrifice everything for their drug or alcohol addictions? Not much, and this shows the harm that can come from all kinds of addictive behavior. Thankfully, most people never reach this stage, but there will always be a number of people who will destroy themselves because of their addiction. For the rest, however, there is a lot that can be done to bring about change and improve the quality of life if only they understand what is at stake. It is never too late for people to make drastic changes in their behavior, but often they sacrifice much of their future happiness before changes are made.

Addiction Defined

All kinds of definitions exist for addiction. One of the most common is that in addiction one is given over to some activity. A more restrictive meaning is that addiction is a harmful involvement with drugs that produces either withdrawal symptoms or tolerance (Alexander & Schweighofer, 1998). These definitions are inadequate because addiction entails more than being given over to an activity, and many activities involve things other than drugs. For the purposes of this book, the best and most practical definition is as follows: An addiction is a compulsion to do something despite the negative consequences. It is not just a compulsion, or a compulsion involving drugs and alcohol, but the giving in to any compulsive behavior despite the negative consequences, and the consequences are of such nature that they lower the quality of life. This definition eliminates the need to distinguish between good and bad compulsions, or to focus on some biological process that is actually the result of an addiction rather than the cause. By definition, addictions involve individual behavior rather than biological disease or some external force. Notice that the compulsion is to *do* something.

So, why in the world would someone want to do something that they know is going to harm them? People usually do not set out with the intention of bringing harm to themselves. The harm occurs after a long process of decision-making that involves individual values, self-perception, environment, and self-deception. It is not just a matter of weak will because some addicts are very strong willed people who are willing to continue a pattern of destructive behavior despite all of the hardship it brings them.

There are many reasons why people choose addiction. Many are unhappy with their own self-perceptions and they use drugs as a way to view themselves differently. Some see unpleasant things in their environment and they use addiction as a way to escape. Addiction often involves values that are different from the mainstream in society. For example, people may value certain behaviors more than they value a job, family, career, money, relationships, and even self-respect. People may also value immediate gratification over anything that might be in the future. Values are a personal matter, and some people do not value health, job, home, family, and financial security more than drugs. It is not that they do not want these things, they just do not value them more than their continuing behaviors. Perhaps they have never really thought through the issue of whether it is in their own best interest to deny themselves some immediate gratification for a future benefit. If so, this would provide an excellent counseling strategy for recovery. Many have already thought this through, however, and their choice is to continue in their behaviors and not think of the future. Or, they foolishly believe that they will escape the negative consequences of their behaviors. When these consequences become apparent, many discontinue their addictions while others do not stop until they are physically unable to engage in the addictive behaviors.

Feelings and Compulsions

We have many compulsions, and not all of them have negative consequences for us. Breathing is one. Some people have compulsions to count things. I had a friend once who loved to count the number of a certain brand of automobile he would see in one day. Sometimes I joined with him in the counting as well and we would compare notes. For this to be labeled an addiction, it would have to be demonstrated that the counting had a negative impact on his quality of life. Even then, it might be a judgment call as to what is negative and what is not. This behavior might appear odd to some, but only because they cannot appreciate the joy of counting things. So, compulsive behavior alone is not an addiction.

Addiction always involves beliefs and behaviors. Addictive behavior may have biological consequences for some people, but biology does not cause addiction. Even if it could be proven that someone had a biological predisposition to engage in certain kinds of behavior, the behavior is still a choice. The physical and psychological states produced by drugs and alcohol are no more powerful than other feelings, desires, and compulsions that people have. For example, falling in love, gambling, hobbies, working, and accumulating possessions can be just as intense, irrational, and self-destructive for some people as any drug habit. Love is such a strong emotion that it can have many of the characteristics of a mental disorder. Because of love, people may lose touch with reality, imagine things, become physically ill, depressed, or even violent. In extreme cases, people take their own lives because of their feelings of love. Yet, no one would suggest that people do not really have a choice in the matter, or that biology, brain waves, or genes force people to behave in certain ways when they are in love. Just as some people refuse to act responsibly when they fall in love, others refuse to act responsibly when they consume drugs, alcohol, or gamble.

A compulsion to gamble, watch television, or count cars does not create a physical dependency, but it may create a psychological dependency. Psychological dependence is when we believe that we must do something to think, feel, or function normally. People develop a physical dependence on drugs when the tissues of the body require the presence of the drug to function normally. Some people continue to increase the amount of the drugs they consume because they have become dissatisfied with the intensity of their drug experience. Tolerance develops when more and more of the drug is required to produce the same effect. It is possible to develop both a physical and a psychological dependence on the chemical substances in drugs, and both physical and psychological dependence can be overcome when people believe it is in their own best interest to do so. People do not go berserk, crazy, or die simply because they deprive themselves of some enjoyable behavior; instead, they long for it like others who desire things they cannot have.

There is a school of thought that divides the definition of addiction to positive and negative components with the goal of steering people toward positive addictions. However, this tends to confuse people about the real nature of addiction. The crucial issue regarding any behavior is the extent to which the negative consequences degrade the quality of one's life, which means that even positive behaviors can have negative consequences if taken to an extreme. For example, a husband and father who works hard at his job is doing a good thing and being responsible; however, if his devotion to work destroys his health or causes him to neglect his family, then it can have negative consequences. It is not the work that is the problem, but an excessive devotion to work that brings harm to oneself and others. To illustrate, my self-employed son, Joey, finds it difficult to take off from work and relax with his family because of his compulsion to work, but the reason he feels anxious when not working is because he is the sole support of his wife and children. Now, this would not make any difference to some men, but my son values his family so much that it causes him to feel uncomfortable when he is not providing for their financial needs. On the other hand, he makes a point to take off occasionally to spend time with his family. So, it becomes a matter of judgment for him as to when he says "No" to his compulsion to work and "Yes" to his compulsion to take off from work to be with his family. There can be negative consequences to both working too much and to taking off too much and it is a matter of judgment as to how this is balanced.

In contrast, the life of a drug addict is completely out of balance and this is why the addict's behavior is so harmful to himself and others. The key to bringing balance to one's life is values. In my son's case, he values both work and leisure. He is continually challenged with the choice of deciding how much to take off from work without getting his life out of balance. His solution is to balance both work and leisure by delegating an appropriate time for each. His goal is to reduce the negative consequences of both working and leisure as much as possible while at the same time enjoying the benefits of both.

How is it possible to bring the right values and balance to people's lives? We cannot force people to adopt our values and bring balance to their lives, which is why I am opposed to forced intervention treatment programs. Your intentions may be good, but change should be voluntary. Your job as a relative, friend, minister, or counselor is to help people discover for themselves what is in their own best interest and to be supportive when change is attempted. Here is where faith and religion can be of help. People who are actively involved in their religion can find the values, support, and direction necessary to overcome their addictions.

In the city where I live, the unemployment rate is one of the lowest in the nation, yet I often see able-bodied young men standing on the street holding up signs that say something like: "Will work for food." Most of the time they are not really interested in working, they just want you to give them some money. Some are willing to work to earn just enough to buy some food or drugs, but they do not want a steady job because this would require them to give up their free lifestyle. Right now, they value their drug use and freedom more than they value the benefits that come with a regular job. At this point in their lives, they feel that the negative consequences of holding a job and being responsible are greater than the negative consequences of being free and using drugs. Just because the judgment they make may not be one that you would make does not mean that you have the right to impose your values on them.

We should allow people the freedom to make their own choices regarding their lives and not force intervention on those who are not interested, but neither should we feel obligated to assist them in their current lifestyle. I never respond to able bodied men who hold up signs asking for gifts because this would be enabling them in their irresponsibility. They have a right not to work and to use drugs, but I have the right not to support them in their addictions.

Uppers, Downers, and All Arounders

Some drugs are legal, like caffeine, nicotine, and alcohol, while other drugs are illegal, like marijuana, heroin, and cocaine. Some drugs are only legal if we can get a doctor to prescribe them. There is nothing intrinsically good or evil about drugs, and society and culture determine what is legal and illegal.

For an excellent review of the different drugs and their use, see Inaba and Cohen (2004). Their book is aptly titled, *Uppers, Downers, All Arounders: Physical and Mental Effects of Psychoactive Drugs*, which is a convenient way to remember the main classifications and general characteristics of drugs. Uppers are stimulants, downers are depressants, and all arounders are hallucinogens.

Uppers stimulate the central nervous system and make the consumer feel energetic, alert, confident, and even aggressive. Some stimulants are found naturally in plants like coffee (caffeine) and tobacco (nicotine) while others are synthesized, like methamphetamines. A familiar brand name synthetic stimulant is Ritalin, which is prescribed by doctors for a number of reasons. Why do people want to use stimulants? Stimulants can boost energy and give the individual a feeling of power. They can also depress the appetite and cause weight loss, which is one of the reasons people take stimulants. For example, the fear of weight gain is an argument that cigarette smokers often give for not wanting to quit.

Caffeine in coffee and some soft drinks is often used by people to give them energy to start the day. I have heard people say, "I just can't get going in the morning without a cup of coffee." Once a routine like this is established, a person begins to develop psychological and physical dependence on stimulants to feel and function normally. Many people use caffeine, nicotine, amphetamine, or cocaine to give them the energy to make it through their work day. The body, however, can become depleted of its energy over time, and more and more of the drug is required to receive the same effect. This is not a natural process for the body and it eventually produces negative effects, including a physical collapse and periods of depression. It is possible that large doses of stimulants can cause people to imagine things and become paranoid. For example, I once had a client who experienced a psychotic episode after consuming six diet Pepsis over a period of a few hours. Although this man had a history of abusing cocaine and other drugs, it was likely the caffeine in his soft drink that triggered his psychosis.

Downers depress the central nervous system. They can cause relaxation and feelings of euphoria. Three major depressants today are alcohol, opioids, and sedatives. Opioids, which are good at relieving pain, come from the opium poppy and can be refined to different forms such as morphine, codeine, and oxycodone. OxyContin is the brand name of an excellent pain reliever derived from oxycodone, but because it has been targeted for abuse by some people, this drug is now viewed as dangerous. As a result, many doctors are hesitant to prescribe it and many pain sufferers are afraid to take it. However, there is really nothing wrong with OxyContin, and the negative reputation this drug has developed in the last few years is a good example of blaming the drug for bad behavior.

The most abused depressant in America today is alcohol. Although alcohol is a legal drug, more than 100,000 deaths a year in the United States can be attributed to alcohol (Fisher & Harrison, 2000), which is far greater than the damage done by illegal opiods like heroin. Other negative consequences of alcohol addiction are decreased work productivity, work absenteeism, school truancy, birth defects, and financial loss. Alcohol is often a major factor in family violence, sexual assault, and other criminal acts. In 2001, about 40% of motor vehicle deaths in the United States involved alcohol (Inaba & Cohen, 2004).

Depressants are consumed for a variety of reasons. People turn to depressants to help them relax, go to sleep, temporarily escape from problems, reduce worry, develop feelings of euphoria, lose inhibitions, gain confidence, or find relief from pain. Some depressants can also be used as muscle relaxants. Depressants can be used to aid sleep and many are available for purchase over-the-counter without a prescription (for example, Nytol and Sominex).

All arounders are drugs that affect the mind and perception of the senses. They can also cause a person to hallucinate. All arounders are sometimes called psychedelic drugs. There are several classifications and many different kinds of psychedelic drugs. Some of the most familiar are LSD and PCP. Many of these drugs are derived from plants like marijuana, peyote, and mushrooms. For a more detailed listing, see Inaba & Cohen (2004). Hallucinogens affect thinking and perception. Their use can cause anxiety, paranoia, and psychosis.

All Drugs are Drugs

In his 1972 book, *The Natural Mind*, Andrew Weil makes this important observation about drugs, "I would like to see all of who use legal drugs—caffeine, nicotine, alcohol—to begin seeing these substances for the drugs they are and their habitual use for the addictions they are" (198). We tend to think that legal drugs are not as addictive and are safer to use than illegal drugs. This is not necessarily the case because people can be addicted to just about any drug, regardless of whether it is legal, illegal, prescription, nonprescription, synthetic, or natural. A drug is a chemical substance that has a particular effect on the body. For a variety of reasons, many people desire the psychological and physical effects these drugs provide. The real issue, however, is not the drugs, or the power of drugs, but the reasons why people seek some altered state of consciousness. Interestingly, almost all drugs that are illegal today were at one time legal. For example, cocaine was once used to combat hunger and fatigue in combat soldiers. It was also an ingredient in Coca-Cola soft drinks, which gave Coke its name.

I grew up and went off to college in the decade of the 60s, which has been portrayed as the beginning of the drug culture, or a time when drug use began to accelerate in America. It is more likely, however, that there was not really an increase in drug use during this time but a switch from legal drugs, like nicotine and alcohol, to illegal drugs. For example, in the rural school district where I attended high school, the drugs of choice were nicotine and alcohol. I do not recall ever seeing or hearing of anyone who used any other drug.

As a society, we go through periods where we are fascinated with the use and abuse of certain drugs. Alcohol, for example, was consumed in greater amounts per person during the colonial period of America than it is today. Cocaine has been around for a long time, but the smokable form of cocaine that appeared in the early 1980s popularized this drug with large numbers of people. At that time, I heard stories about how crack cocaine was so addictive that it was going to take over America. This drug was said to be so potent that once you started taking it you lost all control and could never stop. The predicted crack cocaine take-over, however, never happened and the addictive powers of cocaine were largely overstated at the time (Erickson & Alexander, 1998; Fingarette, 1998). Instead, it was discovered that cocaine is no more addictive than other chemical substances that are abused by a minority of people.

Today, we hear of other drugs, like methamphetamine. Methamphetamine, which is a derivative of amphetamine, is a powerful stimulant that affects the central nervous system. The drug gives increased energy and alertness and decreases the appetite. I remember working with a meth addict who took the drug so she could work two jobs and not feel tired. It would be nice to have this much energy, and I can see why someone might want to feel this way, but this does not make the drug irresistible.

So, what is the most serious drug problem in America today? It is the same today as it has been for over one hundred years: nicotine and alcohol. Although most recognize the problems caused by illegal drugs today, many fail to recognize that more harm to health is done by legal drugs than by illegal drugs. Consider, for example, that about one fourth of adults in the United States continue to smoke cigarettes despite the clear evidence of the damage nicotine does to the heart and lungs.

About one in ten adults in this country has significant health and life problems due to alcohol consumption. The leading cause of death among adolescents and younger adults involve events associated with the use and abuse of alcohol. Some examples are accidents, suicide, criminal activity, violence, and homicides. Although tobacco kills at least twice as many people each year as alcohol, alcohol abuse accounts for more than ten times the deaths from all illegal drugs combined. (For more information on the negative impact of drugs in our society, see the summaries in Fisher & Harrison, 2000; Inaba & Cohen, 2004; and Beck, Newman & Liese, 1993).

Acting Like Pharisees

As a society, we often act like Pharisees regarding drugs. In the New Testament, the Pharisees were known for preaching one thing and practicing something else. Concerning their hypocrisy, Jesus said, "But do not do what they do, for they do not practice what they preach" (Matthew 23:3). Later in the chapter, he says, "You strain out a gnat but swallow a camel" (v. 24). As a nation, we often do not practice what we preach regarding the control of drugs. We legalize and consume the drugs doing the most harm to our society while we put people in jail for merely possessing less harmful drugs. We focus on the illegal drugs while neglecting the weightier matters—nicotine and alcohol.

Another inconsistency in our society is that we often do not appreciate the danger of other addictions, like gambling, where the negative consequences can be quite serious. For example, one survey of gamblers revealed that 19% had experienced bankruptcy. The average household debt for this group was $48,000 compared to $22,000 for those who did not gamble. In addition, problem gamblers have higher rates of arrest and incarceration, divorce, and greater physical and mental health issues than non-gamblers (Ciarrocchi, 2002).

I once heard a story of a young man who loved to fish. He not only spent all of his spare money and time on his hobby, he also began to buy things he could not afford, like a nice bass boat. Eventually, his hobby caused him to neglect his family, job, and finances. This young man's lack of control over his compulsive spending and hobby resulted in negative consequences for himself and others. Although he claimed to be religious, his manner of life indicated that his hobby was more important than his faith, family, friends, finances, job, and future happiness. This man did not gamble or use drugs, but the value he placed on his hobby caused him to neglect other things important to his happiness. Yet, many would argue that this man did not have an addiction, or that his addiction was not as serious as an addiction to drugs.

All addictions require an exchange of some kind. People are often unaware of the exchange they have made, or of the consequences of the choices they make. With all kinds of addictions, the negative consequences tend to cause more harm than expected.

The Moral Model

Today, there is almost a universal resistance to attaching any moral culpability to addiction. There are many reasons for this, chief of which is the influence of the disease model of addiction and Alcoholics Anonymous (AA) where addicts are told, "You're not bad, you're sick." Since the disease model labels addiction as a sickness rather than a behavior, people retain a certain innocence regarding their behaviors. For example, you cannot say someone is bad just because they happen to get sick. Instead, the impression is left that you should accommodate addicts in their sickness as you would someone who has the flu or cancer.

Cognitive and choice approaches also prefer to reject the "moralistic rhetoric" of religion (Schaler, 1998, 239). Although these approaches reject moralistic rhetoric, they nevertheless accept the idea that people are accountable for their behavior. Their argument is that addiction is bad in the sense that people harm themselves and others by their irresponsible behavior. The choice approach argues that people can change if they want to, and the power to change resides in humankind. But how different is this from the moral model? There is not really any difference except for some religious terminology like the words God and sin.

But what about the moralistic rhetoric of judging people as bad? Some of this is due to the misuse of both religion and biblical teaching by a few people who talk about addiction. More often than not, the source of the anxiety relative to the moral model is rooted in an inordinate fear that religion will be imposed on those who are not religious. These fears are rooted in a misconception of both biblical Christianity and religion in America. There is no secret Christian jihad taking place in America today that has as its goal the forced conversion of unbelievers. In contrast, biblical conversion is always based on the willing acceptance of the gospel message (Acts 2:41). When religious people speak of faith, morals, and right and wrong, they are usually speaking from the perspective of their own Christian faith. There is nothing in biblical literature to suggest that Jesus ever intended that his followers force people to conform to biblical norms, and if this has ever been done in world history it was a violation of the teaching and spirit of biblical Christianity. To speak about the morality of certain behaviors is not the same as trying to forcibly impose a value system on others. The Bible does not require Christians to do this and actually teaches against it. For example, Paul told the church at Corinth that they should not discipline those who were outside of the church, "I have written you in my letter not to associate with sexually immoral people—not at all meaning the people of this world who are immoral, or the greedy and swindlers, or idolaters" (1 Corinthians 5:9-10). In the next verse he says it only applies to "anyone who calls himself a brother" (v. 11). So, the moral argument is only applicable to those people who are in agreement with the moral values in question. Whether the subject is religion or addiction, people should not be forced to change their beliefs or their behaviors. For some, however, religion itself is the real offense of the moral argument. Rather than denigrating religion, it is better to use the moral authority of faith as an incentive to change for those who believe.

What many seem to be afraid of with the moral argument is the injection of religion and morality into drug treatment, but religion is already there in the guise of the Higher Power in the Twelve Steps theory of addiction treatment. It is the elephant in the room that no one sees! Not only is religion attached to this treatment philosophy, it is often forced on people by judges and counselors who subscribe to the disease model of addiction. Because the disease model rejects the moral model, it is made palatable to the secular mind even though it is a religious approach to addiction treatment.

It is understandable that treatment professionals do not want to interject religion in addiction therapy. The client-therapist relationship does not permit the therapist to impose religious values on clients. The role of the therapist is to help clients find their own solutions to addiction rather than ordering a specific course of action. This seems to work better with people because change is more likely to occur if they decide for themselves what is in their own best interest. This is also the best approach for religious clients as well. It has been my experience that even nominally religious people know when they have messed up their lives and that God is not happy with them. They really do not need to be told. Now, if they ask for advice, or for information, I am always happy to tell them what has worked for me, but this kind of self-disclosure is always in the context of helping people discover their own solutions. To adopt the moral model, therefore, does not require that counselors preach to clients, or impose their own solutions or their own set of values. The place for preaching is in the practice of religion, and in this context, preaching can provide a wonderful resource. Biblical preaching is the food that provides spiritual growth and can inoculate people from addiction and all kinds of irresponsible and harmful behaviors.

One of the benefits of the moral model of addiction is that it refutes the idea that people are at the mercy of their environments, genes, culture, or some other deterministic force. For example, it is beneficial to know that certain behaviors are bad, wrong, or even sinful. Because of faith, many individuals come to realize they have choice, self-control, responsibility, and culpability regarding their behavior. For those who accept the moral model of biblical Christianity, the recognition that behavior is bad, wrong, or sinful can be a strong preventative as well as an incentive to change.

Having acknowledged that the moral model is only relevant when there is an agreement on a common set of values, it is important to note the inconsistency of those who seem so adamant in rejecting any beneficial use of the moral model. As a society, we tend to label behaviors as good or bad and right and wrong. For example, people go to jail all the time because of the use and possession of illegal drugs. We also restrict the use and possession of other drugs, like alcohol and nicotine. Our society now views it as bad or wrong to make these drugs available to children, but when I was in high school, students could openly consume nicotine on school grounds. This seems strange today, but it was common then, which shows that cultural values and norms change over time.

The medical community has encouraged society not to allow people free access to some pain killers and other drugs that might help people with illnesses. As a result, society has decided that it is wrong to make these drugs available without a prescription, and both doctors and patients can be punished if these rules are violated. We also have certain rules about being under the influence of both legal and illegal drugs when operating a vehicle. Religious people may have a value system that is based on a set of biblical values, but society in general has a value system based on its own set of values. Further inconsistency results when, on the one hand, our society in general accepts the disease model of addiction, but on the other hand, punishes people for their addictive behaviors. If addiction is a disease, why punish someone for being sick?

Biblical Morality

The criteria for the moral model of biblical Christianity is found in the books of the New Testament. If we rely on our subjective feelings, regardless of whether it is about addiction or religion, then we are not looking at the moral model of biblical Christianity. This model is objective in nature; that is, it is the same for everyone. Some reject the objective nature of biblical morality by saying that the Bible is always subjectively interpreted as in the saying, "one interpretation is as good as another." Those who argue this way, however, are actually saying that the Bible contains no objective truth that is meaningful, which means that the Bible is of no practical value for today. In contrast, the Bible should be viewed as a moral model for living that can be applied to all people alike in all situations. For those who believe the Bible, it is not only the way of salvation but a way of life, which is why Christians called their movement "the Way" (Acts 19:9; 24:14).

People are often reluctant to be governed by the norms of Scripture. Even some religious people seek ways to escape the application of Scripture to their lives, as the example of some Pharisees in the gospels illustrate. In the Bible, Paul speaks of some Christians who assumed the grace of God allowed them to do as they pleased, "What shall we say, then? Shall we go on sinning so that grace may increase? By no means! We died to sin; how can we live in it any longer?" (Romans 6:1-2). The question "Shall we go on sinning so that grace may increase?" is probably based on some kind of slogan some of the Christians used to justify their unwillingness to change their behavior. Their argument would be something like this, "This is just the way I am, I can't help it" or "Forgiving me is what the grace of God is for." As a result, these Christians expected God to accommodate them in their sinful behaviors by increasing his grace. Paul's response is, "By no means!"

There were other slogans some Christians used to excuse bad behavior, such as the ones given by some Christians at Corinth, "Everything is permissible for me" and "Food for the stomach and the stomach for food." Paul's response, however, is that we should "not be mastered by anything" (1 Corinthians 6:12-13). Freedom in Christ means that we should not be mastered, enslaved, or overpowered by anything.

Jesus said, "If anyone would come after me, he must deny himself and take up his cross and follow me" (Mark 8:34). There are two things taught in this verse relative to addictive behavior. First, self-denial is possible. To follow Christ, disciples can and must deny themselves all kinds of gratification that is not in keeping with the lifestyle of Christ. In contrast, addiction makes the self the center of everything, which is incompatible with the Christian lifestyle. Second, the idea of taking up a cross indicates that we are to live in the way of the cross, as when Jesus bore his own cross, or when Simon from Cyrene was enlisted to bear Jesus' cross (Luke 23:26). Cross bearing suggests that the choice one is asked to make regarding Christian behavior is not always an easy choice. Addiction is also a choice, although it may not be an easy choice.

Conclusion

A strong compulsion to do something is not an addiction. An addiction is a compulsion to do something despite the negative consequences. There is not a biological cause of addiction although behavior can affect human biology. Even if there were a biological predisposition to behave in certain ways, people still have a choice about their behaviors. All drugs are drugs, whether they are legal, illegal, prescription, over-the-counter, or non-prescription. As a society, we are sometimes hypocritical in the way we allow the use of some drugs, like alcohol and nicotine, while making other drugs illegal. The misuse of any drug is a behavior that involves choice, and our lives can easily get out of balance if we choose to abuse drugs. The moral argument is a good incentive for people of faith to stop using drugs and get their lives back in balance.

Recommending Reading

The best overall book on drug use in America is *Uppers, Downers, All Arounders: Physical and Mental Effects of Psychoactive Drugs* by Inaba and Cohen (2004). The authors give a fair and balanced approach to the different drugs being abused today as well as an excellent historical perspective. The title of their book represents the three main classifications of drugs and explains it in such a way that those who are unfamiliar with drugs and addiction can understand the subject. Probably the best book on a history of drug treatment in America is *Slaying the Dragon* by William White (1998). Both of these books give the reader a good overall historical and cultural context of drugs and addiction in the United States.

Questions for Discussion

1. Why is behavior not an addiction when there are no negative consequences? Who gets to decide whether a consequence is negative?
2. Discuss the role that values play in addiction. What role did values play in Melba's decision to stop smoking cigarettes?
3. Is addiction an involuntary behavior or choice about values?
4. What are the similarities between the moral model and the cognitive view of behavior as a choice? In both instances, who gets to determine what is moral and what is a responsible choice?
5. Does the church have an obligation to impose values on those who are not Christians? If not, what is the biblical plan for spreading moral values?

Chapter 2

Spirituality and Addiction

Jack and Jill

One Sunday, a middle aged man named Jack visited the church where I preach. After worship service, Jack asked me if he could come by my office for a visit the next day. During our visit together, I learned that he had spent most of his adult life abusing alcohol. Jack wanted to tell me about his life—about how he had given himself over to alcohol and about his journey back to sobriety. He did not want me to help him stop drinking because he had already done that; instead, he just wanted to tell me about his renewed faith in God and his decision to change his life. According to his story, it all happened one night while he was searching for something to listen to on the radio. He discovered a religious program that he remembered hearing as a young man, and as he listened to the message, he began to think about all that had happened in his life because of his addiction. As he continued to listen, he experienced an emotional and spiritual crisis. With tears of sorrow for a wasted life, he vowed that he would stop drinking and return to his religious roots. His moment of awakening was very emotional as he sensed the loss his addiction had brought to his life. It seems that this was the first time that he truly realized just how out of balance his life had become. All at once, Jack had insight to his condition and was motivated enough to change his behavior. From that moment on, Jack quit drinking and started back to church. His life now was totally different.

Jill was never religious and did not grow up in a Christian home. Through the process of time, she made some choices about her life that led her down the path of drug abuse. Jill never felt that she had a bright future. The more she focused on drugs, the less she had to live for, so she became more and more addicted to drugs. One day, Jill found herself in an empty apartment with no money, no job, no food, and no drugs. At the time, her drug of choice was crack cocaine, but without money, she could no longer buy her drug. She began to search the apartment for small amounts of crack cocaine that may have dropped on the floor. As she was on her hands and knees, pulling apart the carpet fibers in search of her drug, she had a psychological and spiritual experience. She suddenly gained insight to her miserable condition and found the motivation to change. She said to herself, "I do not want to live this way anymore." Jill made a change in her thinking, motives, and values and she turned her life around. She did not call on a Higher Power, start going to church, experience a religious conversion, admit to herself that her life was unmanageable, or confess that she was helpless to do anything about her addiction. Instead, Jill just decided to live differently.

Both Jack and Jill had life changing experiences that enabled them to make dramatic and permanent changes. Their stories are typical of many who quit serious addictions. I would argue that both of them experienced a psychospiritual crisis that resulted in dramatic change, but only one experience had something to do with God, religion, or the Bible. Jack returned to the religion of his youth for support and Jill formed a different set of values for her life. In both cases, the spiritual experience provided the necessary insight and motivation for change. Both had a moment of awakening that allowed each of them to stand outside of themselves and view the world more objectively. This experience gave each of them the insight and motivation to make a dramatic change. Not all change is this dramatic, or accompanied by an emotional and spiritual crisis. Some people change gradually over time and have many setbacks along the way, but others change all at once after discovering new insight and values following some kind of spiritual experience.

There is a lot of confusion today about spirituality and religion in the treatment of addiction. Why is it that some people are able to suddenly stop their addiction while others seem incapable of doing so? What are these change experiences that people have? Are they spiritual, psychological, religious, emotional, or all of the above? Words can have different meanings in different contexts. It is easy to see how someone might think of these experiences as being religious, especially if they are called spiritual experiences. However, spiritual insight is not limited to religion and can exist outside of religion.

The goal of this chapter is to work through the definition of some important terms in such a way that we can avoid the misunderstandings that people have about addiction and change. This task is made more difficult because some treatment programs claim to be spiritual but have religious components, while others claim to reject spirituality because they believe it is religious. Another goal is to discover the difference between religion and spirituality by defining each in such a way that each definition can stand alone.

Religion and Spirituality

Alcoholics Anonymous, with its Twelve Steps treatment program, claims to be spiritual rather than religious, but aspects of the Twelve Steps theory appear to be religious to many. For example, the belief in a Higher Power, individual helplessness, confession of wrongs, and developing a moral inventory all appear to be religious in the common sense understanding of the terms. Yet, AA adamantly denies any connection to religion. For the most part, this has allowed the Twelve Steps theory to escape the scrutiny of those who oppose the mixture of religion and drug treatment. How is it possible, then, to tell the difference between religion and spirituality, and is there really any difference between the two terms? The goal of this chapter is to differentiate between religion and spirituality so that spirituality can be used in addiction treatment without becoming religious. Twelve Steps theory has not successfully done this, and the efforts to distinguish between religion and spirituality have only watered down the religious aspects of AA and Twelve Steps.

The separation of AA from religion has allowed the treatment program to join with the medical community's disease approach to addiction. Since the 1930s an effort has been made to promote the disease connection to alcohol abuse and more recently the application has been made to other behaviors. As a result, an unusual alliance between religion and medicine began in the 1940s and continues to the present. The disease model approach to behavior and the religious aspects of the Twelve Steps theory were not seriously challenged until the work of Peele (1989), Fingarette (1998), and Schaler (2000). Today, the disease concept of addictive behavior is seldom questioned by the general public because of its connection to many in the medical community. Treatment programs for behaviors other than alcohol and drug abuse have generally followed variants of the Twelve Steps theory while the medical community has obliged by also labeling these behaviors as diseases. In response to the charge of being a religious treatment approach, many point out that AA is just a support group and not a treatment program. However, the Twelve Steps theory involves 12 steps of treatment and this program is advocated by AA.

The efforts of AA and the Twelve Steps theory proponents to water down their religion by making it universalistic does not solve the problem. Religion is religion, and whether it is specific in nature as in biblical Christianity, or universal as in some vaguely defined Higher Power, it still offends those who are not looking for a religious-based treatment program. This becomes especially offensive when drug courts order secular addicts to enter a religious-based treatment program. It is also offensive to religious people who happen not to agree with the kind of religion promoted in the Twelve Steps theory.

Spirituality and religion must be defined differently for the benefit of both believers and non-believers. In discussing religion, I make no attempt to include or describe the different religions of the world, or even all of the religions that wear the name Christian. Instead, religion is defined in terms of biblical teaching, which means I occasionally cite passages from the Bible to illustrate biblical teaching.

Spiritual capacity and insight is a part of personhood, and has been given by God to all humankind in creation. Perhaps it is a part of being created "in the image of God" (Genesis 1:27). Just as humans have been created with many capabilities, such as sight, smell, hearing, cognition, and mobility, humans also have a spiritual component that they can use in times of need. Although the spiritual capacity in humans is not religious, it is an important aspect of biblical religion.

Both religion and spirituality can be helpful in addiction recovery. Those who come from a biblical perspective recognize spirituality as a vital part of biblical religion, but spirituality, properly defined, is a human capacity that exists in contexts other than religion. One of the problems in addiction treatment is the blurring of these two concepts. For example, although the Twelve Steps theory insists it is spiritual and not religious, it nevertheless defines spirituality in religious terms. The better way is to define spirituality in a way that is separate from religious terminology and concepts. This is not a secularization of religion, but a simple recognition that humankind has a spiritual capacity that is beneficial to both religion and addiction treatment. The goal now is to formulate a more precise definition of both religion and spirituality.

A good general definition of religion is that it is an organized social system containing a body of beliefs and practices with a view to some kind of ultimate reality (Ciarrocchi, 2002). This fits nicely with the religion described in the Bible, but a more precise biblical definition of religion would depend on the time period and the covenant under consideration. For example, religion is expressed differently for each of the covenants with Adam (Genesis 3), Noah (Genesis 6), and Abraham (Genesis 17) . These covenants point the way to the grand covenant with Moses and the nation of Israel (Exodus 24:8), which finds its ultimate fulfillment in the new covenant of Jesus Christ (Jeremiah 31:31; Matthew 26:26-28; John 1:17; Hebrews 8:7-13).

Spiritual Insight

Spirituality is a capacity within humankind that enables people to recognize certain things about themselves, and with some people, this insight provides the motivation for significant change. Spirituality is beneficial because it brings objectivity and clarity to people's lives. Piedmont (1999) calls this spiritual transcendence. "Spiritual transcendence refers to the capacity of individuals to stand outside of their immediate sense of time and place to view life from a larger, more objective perspective" (988). This is a workable definition for both secular and religious contexts. The idea of transcendence is to move beyond oneself with a non-worldly perspective of things. From the teaching of Christ, we learn that people can become so materially focused that they lose perspective of more important things. An example of this lack of insight in Jesus' day was an occasion when a man asked Jesus to settle a financial dispute. Jesus said to the man, "Watch out! Be on your guard against all kinds of greed; a man's life does not consist in the abundance of his possessions" (Luke 12:15). This prompted Jesus to tell a parable about a rich man who focused only on building wealth for himself. At night, he thought about how he could tear down his barns and build bigger ones so that his wealth might increase. Jesus gives us God's response, which reveals the lesson of the parable. "You fool! This very night your life will be demanded from you. Then who will get what you have prepared for yourself?" (v. 20).

The message of the parable concerns this man's total lack of insight to his true situation. He was so blind about his condition that he could not stand outside of his present world to view life from a more objective perspective. That made him a fool in God's sight. God did not create fools just so he could call them fools, so there must be some moral culpability on the part of the rich man for his own blindness. His blindness likely occurred over a long period of time through a process of decision-making that produced the lack of insight about himself and his relationship with God. In a similar way, blindness to the harmful effects of addiction does not occur overnight, or through defective genes or brainwaves, as some suggest. Rather, addiction happens when people do not look beyond themselves or even think very much about what is happening. They cannot shift their focus from the worldly, physical, and immediate impulse, to something meaningful outside of their present environment. The focus is on immediate gratification without any consideration of long-term consequences.

Spiritual transcendence, which is the ability to step outside of one's present circumstance and view life from a different perspective, is an important component of biblical religion. The practice of religion without spiritual insight is often criticized by Jesus:

> Woe to you, teachers of the law and Pharisees, you hypocrites! You give a tenth of your spices—mint, dill and cummin. But you have neglected the more important matters of the law—justice, mercy and faithfulness. You should have practiced the latter, without neglecting the former. (Matthew 23:23)

What is the difference between tithing the smallest of spices, such as the mint, dill, and cummin, and practicing the more important matters of justice, mercy, and faithfulness? The act of tithing is more concrete, and can be done without spiritual insight, but justice, mercy, and faithfulness are more abstract, and require one to view life from the perspective of God. Jesus is not saying they should not have tithed, but that they did not have spiritual insight in their practice of justice, mercy, and faithfulness, which Jesus says is more important than their acts of tithing. Jesus calls this lack of insight blindness (vs. 16-17).

The language of biblical Christianity describes a lack of spirituality as being of the world, or worldly in one's outlook. The Bible says, "For everything in the world—the cravings of sinful man, the lust of his eyes and the boasting of what he has and does—comes not from the Father but from the world" (1 John 2:16). Even some Christians resisted spiritual insight: "Brothers, I could not address you as spiritual but as worldly..." (1 Corinthians 3:1).

What happens in worldliness is that we lose focus on things outside of our own worldly experience. This prevents us from having an objective view of what is happening at the moment. If we cannot develop spiritual insight to our condition, we cannot find God. In a similar way, people often fail to gain insight to their own addictions. Their lives have little meaning and purpose and their focus is on immediate gratification. They seldom recognize the consequences or broader context of their own behaviors. This lack of insight prevents them from identifying the values and solutions that would allow them to change their current behaviors.

Spirituality is the capacity that allows men and women to be both observant and religious in the biblical sense, but it also allows humankind to do other things as well. People who do not believe and are not religious still need the ability to connect with their inner self and develop an awareness that transcends their current worldly view. One of the best insights to human spirituality and the connection to mental health is by psychiatrist Peter Breggin (1991, 1999). Breggin argues that people can have a spiritual crisis when they are faced with anxiety and uncertainty about their present condition. This may result in emotional suffering, expressed in such ways as depression, guilt, anxiety, shame, anger, or emotional numbing. Breggin suggests that mental disorders can often be attributed to the way people respond to a spiritual crisis. To deal with their emotional pain, many people intensify their use of mind altering substances, such as drugs and alcohol, or destructive behaviors that provide emotional escape, such as compulsive gambling. These responses may provide some temporary relief, but no long-term solution. Eventually, these temporary fixes become an even greater problem, often causing another spiritual crisis as people begin to realize there is something seriously wrong with their lives. The way they handle their spiritual crisis can be either the cause or the solution to their addiction.

Breggin (1991) points out that spirituality refers to "the self, identity, or personality of the individual, including his or her striving to live a better, more fulfilling or meaningful life" (26). Spirituality is the effort to become connected again with the inner self and find meaning and purpose in life. A spiritual crisis can occur when we have feelings of being overwhelmed with our present circumstances. The relevant point for the present discussion is that individuals need spiritual insight before they can make beneficial change, and a lack of insight can result in emotional harm.

A psychospiritual crisis is our mind telling us that something is wrong. Intensifying addictive behavior is an inappropriate response to this crisis. Breggin would argue further that psychotic and neurotic responses are inappropriate as well. A positive response to a spiritual crisis is one that produces changes in thinking and behavior. In addiction, this positive response is often referred to as a moment of awakening.

Spiritual Insight and Dramatic Change

There is no addiction that cannot be changed, and changes can be either dramatic or gradual, depending on the individual and the circumstances. One of the best studies of dramatic change is by Miller and C'de Baca (*Quantum Change*, 2001). In researching their book, the authors interviewed former addicts with a view to finding out why some of them made dramatic changes in their behaviors. They found that dramatic change can best be characterized by insight, "Suddenly the person comes to a new realization, a new way of thinking or understanding" (18). A majority of those who made a dramatic change can recall in vivid detail the exact time and circumstance when they made this decision, as illustrated by the stories of Jack and Jill at the beginning of this chapter. The change results in a major shift in values along with a recognition of the discrepancies in their lives prior to transformation (164). It is the sudden insight to this discrepancy that triggers the change, "In part, quantum change seems to emerge from inner conflict, from a clashing of 'how I am' and 'how I want to be or could be'" (178). This is an example of spiritual insight as defined in this chapter. Spiritual insight is the ability and willingness to transcend the immediate material focus with a view to seeing the total picture. This new spiritual transcendence allows people to get outside of themselves and view life from a more objective viewpoint. The authors even compare this phenomenon to religious conversion, where the individual develops "an inner transformation of the heart, of consciousness" (168). Although this experience may have some similarities to religious conversion, it is not necessarily religious.

This compares favorably to what is found in the Bible regarding spiritual insight and dramatic change. A good example of dramatic transformation in the Bible is the story of the lost son (Luke 15:11-23). The son demanded an inheritance from his father so that he could go to a distant place and squander the money in wild living (v. 14). As we read the story, it is easy to identify the son's faulty thinking about his condition. Does he really think it is in his own best interest to do this? Apparently, he does not give it any thought. His focus is only on immediate gratification and he has no insight into the future or his true condition; that is, he is worldly and not spiritual. You would think that no one would be so foolish or so blind! Each time I read this story, however, I am reminded of people I have counseled with over the years. Like the lost son, they acted impulsively without any regard for the negative consequences. It seems never to have entered their minds that they would one day be without health, money, job, family, and friends because of their addiction.

Eventually, the lost son found himself destitute and alone in a pig pen. He was so desperate for food that he "longed to fill his stomach with the pods that the pigs were eating, but no one gave him anything" (v. 16). It was at this moment that he began to have a spiritual crisis. One might call this his moment of awakening:

> When he came to his senses, he said, "How many of my father's hired men have food to spare, and here I am starving to death! I will set out and go back to my father and say to him: Father, I have sinned against heaven and against you. I am no longer worthy to be called your son; make me like one of your hired men." So he got up and went to his father. (Luke 15:17-20)

Notice that this young man seems to be having a psychospiritual crisis regarding his difficult situation. Suddenly, he comes to his senses; that is, he gains insight to his condition and his prior discrepancies ("Father, I have sinned against heaven and against you"). There is a dramatic shift in values, and a clashing of "how I am" and "how I want to be." All of this results in dramatic and immediate change ("I will set out and go back to my father").

This is what spirituality is all about: inner transformation, insight, sensitivity, openness, and an awareness beyond the self. All humankind has this capacity, although it is possible to sear the conscience; that is, negate the consciousness of what is right and wrong. In biblical Christianity, this is described as having one's conscience "seared as with a hot iron" (1 Timothy 4:2), or having futile thinking (Romans 1:21), or being deceived (2 Thessalonians 2:10-11; Galatians 6:7). Therefore, just as one has the ability to gain spiritual insight, one also has the ability to lose insight.

Religion and Addiction Treatment

The recovery group known today as Alcoholics Anonymous was started by two alcohol addicted individuals in 1935. Both of these men felt they were powerless over their addiction:

> Out of this insight was created the AA fellowship, dedicated to the proposition that an alcoholic is unable to control his or her drinking and that only through support and acceptance of those in the same condition can the person achieve sobriety (which requires total abstinence). (Peele, 1989, 43-45)

The founders used the teachings of an ecumenical religious organization called the Oxford Group as a framework to develop their Twelve Steps philosophy of addiction treatment. This philosophy includes ideas of powerlessness, character defect, confession, restitution, and evangelizing others. Peele points out that in the 1940s, the Yale Center of Alcohol Studies collaborated with AA to promote the concept of the disease model of alcoholism (45). The combined influence of these two groups was strengthened in 1960 with the publication of an influential book by E. M. Jellinek titled, *The Disease Concept of Alcoholism*. In this book, Jellinek argues that loss of control is the characteristic that distinguishes those who are addicted to alcohol from those who are not. From this point on, the disease model of addiction has been the dominate view of alcohol abuse treatment. Soon, the disease concept and AA philosophy began to spread to other addictions, including Narcotics Anonymous (1953), Gamblers Anonymous (1957), Overeaters Anonymous (1960), Sexaholics Anonymous (1979), and Nicotine Anonymous (1988), among others.

The Twelve Steps philosophy does not separate spirituality from religion as adherents like to claim. The idea that we are powerless to control our behavior has more to do with the deterministic theology of John Calvin than science, medicine, or effective drug treatment. The idea that one must believe in a Higher Power greater than oneself is a religious concept and regardless of how vaguely defined the Higher Power is, it is still a religious belief. The idea that we have to turn our lives over to a Higher Power, or that we have to do a moral inventory, or that we have to admit to ourselves and others that we have done wrong, or that we should evangelize others regarding our own spiritual awakening is religious ideology. The medical community has felt some discomfort with this, and AA has gone to great lengths to argue that their definition of spirituality is not religious, but the elements of a religion are all there. As a result, the religion of AA is continually being watered down in an effort not to offend others and to make room for differing religious views. In the end, however, it is still religious. The most harmful aspect of the Twelve Steps theory is not the religion it imposes on unbelievers but the deterministic thinking relative to human behavior, which means it sows the belief in the minds of addicts that they are powerless relative to their addictions.

The religious component of the Twelve Steps treatment has also spread to organizations established to treat other addictive behaviors. For example, Gamblers Anonymous (GA) has a Twelve Steps philosophy composed of character traits, such as honesty, hope, faith, courage, integrity, and service. These are supposed to be the characteristics that represent the highest and finest qualities of humankind. This is all well and good, but is this really necessary to stop an addiction?

Perhaps the reason for the widespread acceptance of the Twelve Steps theory by the medical community is that it fits nicely with their concept of disease treatment. It also allows medical doctors to bill the insurance industry for their services in treating a behavior. The best approach to addiction treatment, however, is to define spirituality in such a way as to separate it from religion. If it is the case that a client has some religious values that would be helpful to addiction recovery, then these can be used for that purpose. Religion can be a powerful and positive force in the recovery process and it can inoculate people from addictive behaviors, but it only works when those who are being treated are in agreement with the religion.

The Bible and the Higher Power

Through the influence of AA and Twelve Steps, America has come to know the value of something called the Higher Power in the treatment of drug and alcohol addiction. For AA and the Twelve Steps treatment model to have a universal appeal, the Higher Power is never clearly defined and can represent anything outside of oneself. Valverde (1998) argues that the meaning of the Higher Power has been so diluted and imprecisely defined as to become meaningless, as in the suggestion that we pray "To whom it may concern" (133). To become more inclusive as a treatment model, the definition can be whatever the addict decides, as long as it is a reliance on something outside of oneself. The Higher Power can be God or gods, Mother Earth, guardian angels, the environmental movement, or some special feeling.

For those who have faith in the God of the Bible, it is better to move away from vague definitions of a Higher Power and accept the definition of God found in creation and the Scripture. An imprecise definition of God is not biblical and is harmful to Christian faith. It also confuses and discourages believers from taking advantage of the practical application of biblical teaching that can enhance recovery efforts.

The argument that humankind is hopeless and helpless to recover from addiction without the direct intervention of something outside of oneself suggests that people are incapable of doing what is in their own best interest, or that they do not have the ability to make common sense choices about their behaviors. It is true that people often do not choose to do the right thing, and the Bible teaches that humankind has a tendency to stray from what is right. For example, the Bible states, "There is a way that seems right to a man, but in the end it leads to death" (Proverbs 14:12). But the fact is, people can and do recover from drug and gambling addictions without appealing to a Higher Power. People also recover without professional treatment, Alcoholics Anonymous, Narcotics Anonymous, Gamblers Anonymous, total abstinence, Twelve Steps, support groups, or religion.

There is no religious requirement for stopping an addiction. Although a religious component can be very beneficial for many believers, it is not a requirement for success, and both believers and unbelievers can do well with a secular and practical approach to recovery along the lines of Peele (2004). This is not to suggest that those who believe the Bible should never look to God for guidance. This is what believers do when they turn to the Bible for help, as Jeremiah says, "I know, O Lord, that a man's life is not his own; it is not for man to direct his steps" (Jeremiah 10:23). Certainly, one can benefit from listening to the advice that God gives in the Bible about how to direct one's life. It is possible that either the Bible or individual spiritual introspection can provide the necessary insight for change. Helpful insight can also occur as the result of visiting with a counselor, religious leader, medical doctor, family member, or friend. Change is difficult, and many people choose not to change, but change is always possible when there is sufficient insight and desire.

It may be possible to reach a point where addiction has destroyed mind, body, and soul to the point that recovery is impossible. Whether this ever occurs is debatable. No one can know with certainty at what point people lose their capacity to change and become permanently given over to drug or alcohol addiction. Even if it is the case, it does not contradict the fact that addiction is a choice, but only shows that we can be deceived and deluded about our condition. This is in harmony with biblical teaching, for the Bible often warns about the consequences of our actions, and how we can be deceived, "Do not be deceived: God cannot be mocked. A man reaps what he sows" (Galatians 6:7). One of the things we can reap is our own destruction (v. 8). The Bible also speaks of the evil that deceives those who are perishing, "For this reason God sends them a powerful delusion so that they will believe the lie and so that all will be condemned who have not believed the truth but have delighted in wickedness" (2 Thessalonians 2:11-12). People do not start deluded and deceived about their behaviors. The Bible says they become deceived and a delusion is sent, suggesting that deception and a delusion are the result of a long process of decision-making.

As mentioned previously, the Twelve Steps theory of loss of control, powerlessness, and the required action of a Higher Power is a religious-based treatment approach that has its religious roots in the ecumenical Oxford Group and the theological determinism of John Calvin. These deterministic features are present in the treatment methods of AA, Twelve Steps, and the disease model. In fairness, the disease model does not have its roots in religion but in the biological nature of disease, which is also deterministic in that we cannot choose to get sick. Because these two views of behavior share a common philosophy, they join together in their approach to addiction treatment. The misapplication of determinism to addiction behavior runs counter to the more practical and successful cognitive techniques described in Beck (1993), Schaler (2000), Peele (2004), and others. This determinism encourages people to define themselves in negative and self-defeating ways, such as "I am an alcoholic" or "I am an addict," as if this is a part of one's personhood. Note how this kind of confessional dominates in current AA and disease model approaches to addiction. It is not a mistake, or counter to Scripture, to suggest that individuals have choice, willpower, and control over their lives, even when it comes to addiction.

Defining God

Religious and Bible believing people tend to be pleased with the idea of a Higher Power being introduced to addiction treatment, but there is a danger in loosely defining deity and universalizing religion. It is important, therefore, for believers of the Bible to define deity in a way that is in harmony with biblical teaching for both the good of their faith and their recovery from addiction. My purpose now is to define deity in the framework of Scripture.

A crucial highpoint is reached in the Old Testament when Moses received God's law on Mount Sinai, "And he wrote on the tablets the words of the covenant—the Ten Commandments" (Exodus 34:28). In the beginning of these commands, some important rules are given relative to the nature of deity, "I am the Lord your God, who brought you out of Egypt, out of the land of slavery" (Exodus 20:2). What many do not realize is that there is a special name for deity standing behind the English translation of "Lord" in this verse. God is precisely defined by this name as well as his history and relationship with Israel. In the next verse, we are given the first commandment of God, "You shall have no other gods before me" (v. 3). For those who take the Bible seriously, there can only be one God (Deuteronomy 6:4; Mark 12:29). From a biblical standpoint, we cannot, on the one hand, argue that addiction recovery cannot occur unless there is a direct intervention of a Higher Power, and then, on the other hand, accept Mother Earth, Wiccan Religion, pagan gods, and so forth as just another form of the Higher Power. An inconsistency becomes apparent for those who follow biblical teaching by the following dilemma: either intervention by a Higher Power is not necessary for addiction recovery or all of the possible definitions of the Higher Power have equal power with the God of Scripture. What this shows is that intervention by a vaguely defined Higher Power is not really necessary in the first place. Instead, perhaps the God of the Bible created humankind in such a way that people already have the power in themselves to change, and all they need is the insight and motivation to act. A precise definition of God helps those who believe in Scripture see this point more clearly.

From a biblical perspective, it is important to define God in a precise way. Just as spirituality demands that we look beyond ourselves, faith demands that we look beyond the created universe and see the creator behind it. There is evidence that the world did not create itself, and the examination of creation should give us confidence regarding the existence of the creator. Perhaps the greatest evidence that some greater power exists that transcends the world is the idea that there needs to be a first cause for everything. In the real world of our experience, the relationship between cause and effect is self-evident. For every action there is a reaction. There is nothing self-existent in our universe, and experiments in the last century confirmed what was already self-evident to most people—the world had a beginning. If there is a regression of cause and effect in the universe one will eventually arrive at the first cause. This is exactly how Scripture describes it, "In the beginning God created the heavens and the earth" (Genesis 1:1). This beginning stands outside of our present physical universe. It is also outside of space and time. God is the first cause. If someone asks, "Who made God?," then they do not understand what it means to be the first cause. If the God of the Bible can be created, then the God of Scripture is being incorrectly defined.

In the finite world in which we live there cannot be an infinite series of cause and effect events. This is the case because the world is continuing to experience an increase in the series of cause and effect events and it is logically impossible to add to an infinite series of anything. It is possible to have a theoretical infinite series of events but not one that actually exists in the real world. As we begin to work our way back in time we eventually come to the first cause of the first effect that ultimately leads to the world as it exists today. In this exercise, it does not matter whether one is atheist or theist, evolutionist or creationist, secular or religious, the result will be the same. Ultimately one still arrives at the same place, which is the beginning. And now the task is to discover what was there in the beginning. For example, did some non-force take some non-matter and create the present universe? In contrast, the Bible states, "By faith we understand that the universe was formed at God's command, so that what is seen was not made out of what was visible" (Hebrews 11:3). The universe is not composed of finite material and it does not contain anything that is self-existent, pre-existent, or eternal. The universe cannot account for its own existence and the Bible argues that there is evidence in the universe itself that points to a creator, "For since the creation of the world God's invisible qualities—his eternal power and divine nature—have been clearly seen, being understood from what has been made, so that men are without excuse" (Romans 1:20).

God is the one and only self-existent first cause of everything. His eternal power and divine nature are clearly seen through the evidence of creation. As a part of that creation, we should examine ourselves and the rest of creation for evidence of God's work. Looking at creation helps us identify the real God as well as distinguish him from the false gods of our minds. God told Jeremiah to say to Israel, "These gods, who did not make the heavens and the earth, will perish from the earth and from under the heavens" (Jeremiah 10:11). Therefore, we must look to the existence of the universe as a sign of the reality of God, who is the first cause, and the great First Cause of the universe.

Conclusion

Spirituality is a key component of biblical religion, but spirituality and psychospiritual experiences are not confined to religion. Instead, spirituality is God's gift to humankind for the purpose of helping us recognize when something is wrong with our lives. Religious people have nothing to fear from secular treatment approaches such as Beck (1993), Schaler (2000), Miller (2002), and Peele (2004). In general, these approaches are in harmony with and can be supported by religious faith and biblical teaching. The Bible can be used as a source book for reinforcing choice, finding new beliefs, altering one's environment, developing values, and changing problematic behaviors. For people of faith, defining God in more precise terms, and in ways in keeping with the Bible and the known facts of the universe, helps them benefit fully from biblical teaching.

Recommended Reading

Everyone who works in mental health or who has been diagnosed with a mental illness ought to read *Toxic Psychiatry* (1991) and *Your Drug May be Your Problem* (1999) by psychiatrist Peter Breggin. These books give a different view of mental illness as well as point out the danger of using powerful prescription drugs to control some mental health disorders. The author's view of mental disorders is in the context spirituality, psychological overwhelm, and psychospiritual crisis. Mental disorders are often related to substance abuse, and his discussion of spirituality is relevant to understanding addiction and recovery.

Questions for Discussion

1. Discuss the difference between religion and spirituality as defined in this chapter. Why is it the case that these two are often confused?

2. What is it about the Twelve Steps theory that makes it compatible with the medical community's view of disease?

3. Piedmont suggests that spirituality is the ability to stand outside of oneself and view life from a larger and more objective perspective. Discuss how this is significant for religion, mental health in general, and addiction.

4. In the context of spiritual insight, how is tithing different from justice, mercy, and faithfulness?

5. Discuss the similarities and differences between an addict's moment of awakening and religious conversion.

Chapter 3
Religion and Addiction

Easy Button Religion

The call came at just the right time. I had completed most of the writing and research for this chapter but I just could not come up with a good story to illustrate how people misunderstand and misapply religion when it comes to addiction. She had called me at the church office many times before and the request was always the same: "Would you please pray for me." I would always try to be nice and say something like, "Of course, I will put you on our prayer list." I would then try and talk to her about the Bible, her faith, the application of biblical teaching to her life, and her involvement in church. Well, she really wasn't involved in church and had no plans to be involved, but she had all these troubles, and she wanted me to pray for her so that God would help her solve her problems. Her speech was always slurred, mostly incoherent, and just above a whisper. I would often try to get her to help herself, but she did not want to hear that. You see, I was supposed to keep quiet while she told me about her troubles and then I was supposed to ask God to make it better. Anyway, when she called this time I was a little frustrated because, as I said, I was trying to write this chapter. So, instead of spending fifteen minutes on the phone listening to this woman tell me all about her problems, I said, "I will pray for you, you have a nice day, good-bye." However, ten minutes later she called me back. "I called you before," she said, "I want you to pray for me..." And then she began her discussion of how terrible things were for her and that she wanted me to ask God to fix it.

This time I was going to try a different approach. I felt it was time for some hard countering techniques that might help this woman confront her false beliefs about herself so she could deal with the issues in her life. I knew I would run the risk of offending her, but patiently listening to her go on and on about her problems was not doing her any good either, so I bluntly said, "Lady, you can stop abusing drugs and alcohol, it's your choice." You might be thinking, "Isn't this a little off topic?" I strongly suspected, however, that her problems were connected to her drug use, and when she was using, she would get melancholy, and perhaps feel some regret about what she was doing to her life. Then she would call me, and probably a few other preachers in town, in an effort to get some sympathy. No doubt, she wanted me to reassure her that her bad behavior was not her fault, and that God would soon come to her rescue. My firm response, however, was met with silence. There were no protestations or denials, only silence. So, I repeated my earlier statement, "Lady, you can stop abusing drugs and alcohol, it's your choice." This time there was a low inaudible muffling sound of some kind. So, I continued, "I can help you, and God can help you, but if you are not going to help yourself, nothing will ever change. Your addiction is a choice you made, and you can make a choice to stop it. You keep calling here to ask me to call on God to solve your problems, but God is not going to do for you what you will not do for yourself." Our conversation continued along this line for a few minutes and ended with her acknowledgment that God was not going to do for her something that she was able but unwilling to do for herself. At the least, I had given her the opportunity to verbalize a belief that, if she maintained and applied, would result in a dramatic change in her life.

This conversation illustrates how people use and abuse religion. No one is suggesting that the choice about addiction, like many other choices in life, is going to be easy. People often turn to religion with the expectation of finding an easy button solution; that is, just press the button and God solves your problems. Religion is not the only place where these expectations persist. For example, advertisements for weight reduction often suggest that all one has to do is buy a bottle of pills or a certain type of exercise machine to lose weight and look good. In the same way, people want an easy solution for their addictions. The expectations are that if I just stay a month at an expensive treatment center, or follow a few easy steps, or take a certain prescription drug, or see a certain kind of therapist, then I will be healed. The idea is to give up and give in, admit you are helpless, and turn your life over to God or the treatment industry for healing. Yet, I do not find this philosophy of individual helplessness taught anywhere in Scripture. What I find instead is the promise of help and encouragement in doing what is right and a life plan that inoculates you from the common addiction traps.

Some religious people object to this reasoning by pointing out that God has promised to give Christians special help in overcoming addictions that others do not have—thus the rationale for the religious component of Twelve Steps and AA. The problem with this is that one finds too many examples of religious people who remain in addiction despite calling on God for help. As a result, this needlessly disturbs the faith of religious people because they do not see God changing their lives as they were promised. This kind of reasoning is a misunderstanding of how God helps people of faith solve their problems. Another flaw in the Twelve Steps approach is the failure to explain how people of no faith stop their addictive behaviors. This cannot be dismissed by simply saying, "They were never addicted in the first place." This is a convenient way of dismissing reality. Religious people are not the only ones who stop addictions, and secular approaches to addiction treatment like Peele (2004), Miller (2002), Schaler (2000), and Beck (1993) are to be preferred over the disease model and the Twelve Steps approach. In fact, no treatment works for many people because they get tired of the lifestyle and mature out of their addictions. For example, Herbert Fingarette (1998) points out that one third of those addicted to alcohol, including those who are diagnosed as alcoholics, "improve over time without any treatment" (72). This statistic is even higher for those who have a greater support network and a higher socioeconomic status.

Sometimes people argue the Bible teaches that sins and weaknesses like drunkenness are put to death by God in the process of conversion. Therefore all one has to do is be converted and the struggle with addiction ends, or call on God to exercise this power and the addiction goes away. This kind of reasoning is a misunderstanding of Paul's teaching in the book of Romans. In baptism, Paul says that the old man is put to death or done away with and that we have been made free from sin, "For we know that our old self was crucified with him so that the body of sin might be done away with, that we should no longer be slaves to sin" (Romans 6:6). In Christ, the consequences and direction of our sinful tendencies can be put to an end, but the struggle between good and evil continues. In the context of this verse, Paul counters two prevailing thoughts among some early Christians relative to the body and sin. The first group, which characterized the thinking of many Jews and Gentiles in Paul's day, denied that there was a sin problem. Therefore, he spends the first two chapters of the book showing that both groups are under the condemnation of sin. His conclusion is that "Jews and Gentiles alike are all under sin" and "There is no one righteous, not even one" (3:9-10). The second group felt that since the human tendency was to sin, there was no sense in trying to control it. They would argue that the more one sinned, the more God's grace was able to exercise itself on behalf of helpless Christians. Paul's response to this is a rhetorical question: "Shall we go on sinning so that grace may increase? By no means! We died to sin; how can we live in it any longer?" (6:1-2). So, there is no justification for the idea that we are helpless or that we cannot change our behaviors. It would be nice if it were not so, but the Christian is always challenged by behavioral choices. Paul elaborates on this struggle in greater detail in the next chapter (7:7-25). Note the appropriate heading for these verses inserted for this section by the translators of the NIV Bible: "Struggling with Sin." In chapter 6, Paul elaborates on the importance of individual responsibility in putting to death the old self, "Therefore do not let sin reign in your mortal body so that you obey its evil desires" (v. 12) and "Do not offer the parts of your body to sin" (v. 13).

The point of all this is to suggest that there are no easy buttons to push in living the Christian life—it is supposed to be a struggle. Likewise, when people have compulsions to which they give free reign, they should not be surprised that it gets harder and harder to dig out of a hole. This is how free choice works, and Paul is blunt about the consequences of making the wrong choice, "Don't you know that when you offer yourselves to someone to obey him as slaves, you are slaves to the one whom you obey—whether you are slaves to sin, which leads to death, or to obedience, which leads to righteousness?" (v. 16). Addiction to drugs is often pictured as a kind of slavery. For those who go down this path this is certainly the case, but this is true of all behavior. This is the point Paul makes when he says "you are slaves to the one you obey." Yet, the power to enslave is not in the drugs, but in the beliefs and attitudes regarding drugs. Giving in to every compulsion gives only the illusion of freedom, and in the end it always brings slavery. Making excuses for compulsive behavior prevents one from ever finding a remedy. Looking for an easy button solution to addiction is a never ending quest because there are no pain free solutions.

Following the biblical pattern for Christian living means that we must serve a set of biblical values by becoming "slaves to righteousness" (Romans 6:18). This may be too confining for some, but by doing this we learn to master the compulsions that can truly make us slaves. So, learning self-control is the only true path to freedom. This freedom allows us to lead our lives in a productive and meaningful way.

Religion that Helps

As was pointed out in chapter 2, all spirituality is not religious, and all religion does not necessarily involve spirituality. The Bible indicates, for example, that many people fail to make a spiritual application of biblical teaching to their lives. Jesus called people who do this hypocrites, which is a transliteration of a Greek word meaning actor. The idea is that people only pretend to be something, or act the part, because they are not taking their religion seriously. A religion that is not taken seriously is not of much help to those who want to be free of addiction or make other kinds of behavioral changes in their lives.

Before we look at the positive impact religion can have on addiction, let us look in a more general way at the positive impact religious faith can have on physical health and emotional wellbeing. The positive impact of religion on health is usually attributed to improvement in a person's psychosocial factors. Psychosocial is a compound word, containing "psycho," which comes from the Greek word *psyche* and refers to one's mind or beliefs, and "social," which refers to the different ways we relate with other people. So, psychosocial factors refer to those personal beliefs and relationships that impact positively or negatively on our health.

It is often the case that poor relationships are the result of our own attitudes and beliefs about ourselves and others. For example, if we generally have a poor view of others and express our anger easily, it is unlikely that we have a good social network of friends. All of this can lead to social isolation, which tends to encourage negative psychological states like anger, anxiety, and depression. When biblical religion has been internalized, these negative psychological states can be changed for the better, and a natural consequence is that physical health is positively affected. What does all of this have to do with addiction? The point is, addiction prevention and recovery are also affected by positive psychosocial factors.

In general, religion can have many positive effects on people, including improved relationships, peace of mind, better attitudes, reduction of crime, and better physical health. Studies showing the positive relationship of faith and health have had mixed results because religion is not easily defined, and if those who are religious in name only are studied rather than those who have a much greater degree of commitment, then the relation of religion and health may not be apparent. In an attempt to define religious belief and practice, researchers like Spiegel and Fawzy (2002) have tried to differentiate between religion that has been internalized (intrinsic) and religion that is largely in name only or external (extrinsic). Intrinsic religion represents a faith that is reflected in the practices of one's life whereas extrinsic religion may be a religion of convenience or social standing. Beneficial factors, like spirituality, meaning, purpose, hope, and social support, are characteristic of intrinsic religion and produce positive psychological states that are believed to slow the progression of diseases like cancer, whereas negative psychological states are thought to encourage its growth.

The positive effect of intrinsic religion on physical health may have a natural explanation, such as the way it enhances the immune system's fight against diseases (Koenig, 2002), or the health benefits of being in a positive emotional state (Williams, 2002). It could also be a blessing from God like, for example, the promise God made to Israel, "I will take away sickness from among you...I will give you a full life span" (Exodus 23:25). In fact, it could be a combination of all of the above. Since God created humankind, it is reasonable to think that God knows what behaviors and psychological states positively affect health and happiness, and by encouraging us to think and behave in certain ways God is directing us to a healthy and happy lifestyle. These positive factors, along with the avoidance of negative behaviors, are all associated with the lifestyle found in biblical teaching.

Over a generation ago, the foundational work of Friedman and Rosenman (1974) identified the negative effects of hostility and anger on health. In their book, *Type A Behavior and Your Heart*, the Type A behavior describes an emotional style that is generally angry, competitive, hurried, and impatient. The earnest Bible student should recognize immediately how biblical teaching, when internalized and applied, can positively change Type A behavior. Over the years, researchers have built on the work of Friedman and Rosenman by developing a list of psychosocial factors that contribute to illness and early death. Jeff Levin (2001) summarizes this research and attempts to show a connection between religious involvement and the psychosocial factors that positively affect health. For example, his research found that older adults who participate in church activities have lower rates of depression, less anxiety, and live longer than those who are not religious. What is amazing is that this remains true even when taking in account the degree to which religious people tend to avoid unhealthy behaviors, such smoking and drinking.

Mark and Linda Sobell (1993), who are researchers in the field of alcohol dependence, argue that a "sizable proportion of individuals with alcohol problems can solve their problems on their own if they are sufficiently motivated and are provided with some guidance and support" (xi). Religion can provide the incentive for change as well as a support network of other Christians. For Christians, the greatest motivation for change ought to be that the Bible says drunkenness is a sin (1 Corinthians 6:9-10). If alcohol addiction is beyond one's ability to control, then God is asking people to do something that they cannot do, which calls in question the wisdom and truthfulness of Scripture. Yet, as Christians, Paul indicates that we not only have the ability to control our behavior, but the ability to change, "And that is what some of you were" (v. 11).

The moral argument can be a valid tool in the fight against addiction; however, it is only relevant for those who take the Bible and their religion seriously. For those who are not as religious, other cognitive and behavioral approaches work fine, depending on the values and motivation of the client. Although some secular approaches to addiction treatment can be effective, religious people have resources and incentives that can improve their chances of success. When behavior is in conflict with values, a good countering technique is to ask a question, "How do you reconcile your behavior with biblical teaching about drunkenness?" The purpose of pointing out the inconsistency between belief and behavior is not to encourage people to abandon their faith, but to discover an incentive to change.

For those who are actively religious, the church can be the ideal place to find guidance and support. In biblical Christianity, the church is described as a supportive family (Ephesians 3:15; Galatians 6:1-5), and Christians participate in a fellowship in the body of believers (1 Corinthians 12:12). Members of the church family have a responsibility to exhort and encourage one another, "And let us consider how we may spur one another on toward love and good deeds" (Hebrews 10:24). This would be impossible unless Christians met together regularly, which is what the next verse encourages, "Let us not give up meeting together, as some are in the habit of doing, but let us encourage one another..." (v. 25). These regular meetings are supposed to involve worship, association, ministry, and eating together (Acts 2:42-47; 20:7; 1 Corinthians 11:17-33). All of this provides many of the essential ingredients in the prevention of addiction, such as a social support network, individual beliefs and values, and important environmental factors.

Determinism Versus Free Will

To conceptualize the controversy over whether addiction is a choice or a disease, a discussion of the underlying philosophy of each perspective is in order. The disease model, with its belief in irresistible compulsions and loss of control, is in conflict with the choice model, with its belief in individual freedom of choice. In the deterministic model of addiction treatment, behavior is attributed to biology, genes, brainwaves, or sickness, and people do not have free choice about their addictive behaviors. This is sometimes referred to as "loss of control." In contrast, others view humankind as having the ability to make choices, including choices about addiction.

It is important for people to understand the different views regarding human freedom because these views represent the philosophical background of the opposing views in addiction treatment today. What many do not recognize, however, is that the controversy over individual freedom and choice in addiction treatment has roots in a similar controversy in religion, which is why it is important that we now explore the religious history that surrounds the question of whether behavior is predetermined or based on choice. As we explore this religious controversy, notice how many of the terms and ideas are similar to discussions today in addiction treatment.

A debate has existed for more than 500 years among Christian theologians regarding the nature of human freedom. Some view the human condition as one that is fatalistic and predetermined; that is, people do not really have a choice about their salvation or behavior because of their sinful condition. The argument is made that humankind's sinful nature makes one powerless to change behavior or accept salvation without direct intervention by God. This individual powerlessness requires God to act on the heart of each sinner to cure him of his sin problem. The argument is that since God is required to do this before salvation, and since all are not saved, then it must be that God has selected only a certain number to be saved. Furthermore, since God has selected certain ones to be saved, it is impossible for those who have been selected for salvation to act in such a way as to be lost again. This is a simplified overview of religious determinism and one is likely to find many variations. However, what they all have in common is the belief that, to one degree or another, humans are unable to make choices about their behavior or salvation. Others have countered this view by pointing out that God created humankind with the ability to choose right and wrong and to make choices regarding salvation. Those who hold the free will position believe that Scripture teaches that individuals are free to choose and are held to account for the choices they make. For a discussion on this controversy, consult any good history of Christian theology such as, for example, the work by Otto W. Heick (1965).

Philosophers and theologians have argued various forms of determinism over the centuries, but the man who is most responsible for popularizing this view in Christian theology is John Calvin. Although Calvin was active in the 1500s, his views continue to influence the thinking of many Protestant denominations today. Calvin taught that God predetermined what would become of each person. In the *Institutes* Calvin argued, "For all are not created in equal condition; rather eternal life is foreordained for some, eternal damnation for others" (3.21.5). His argument is that some have been predestined to life and some to death; thus, the doctrine of individual predestination. Those who reject Calvin's individual determinism argue that the Bible views election to salvation in a corporate sense rather than an individual sense. For example, Klein (1990) argues that the Bible distinguishes between "God's choice of a corporate people and his choice of individuals who may or may not benefit from that corporate choice" (35).

Calvin's theological determinism can be summarized by the acronym

TULIP. The "T" stands for total depravity. This indicates the individual is incapable of making good choices; therefore, outside intervention must occur to bring the individual to salvation. The "U" represents unconditional election; that is, the individual is saved without any conditions attached to salvation. This means the individual cannot be saved on the basis of whether he chooses to accept God's conditions for salvation because there are no conditions. God makes the choice according to his predetermined plan. The "L" stands for limited atonement, which means that Christ died only for a certain number. This means that salvation is not really for all. The "I" stands for irresistible grace; that is, when God extends his grace to individuals it is irresistible and they are required to accept it. The "P" represents individual predestination, which means that salvation has been foreordained for some but not for others.

Religious determinism has parallels in our culture today. For example, there seems to be a campaign to absolve people of responsibility for their own decisions. We are told that people are not really responsible because they are sick, or they have a disease, which means they cannot help it. Stanton Peele (1989), in his excellent book, *Diseasing of America*, provides a summary of the ways our culture has been avoiding responsibility for behavior because of the disease label. He and other mental health professionals have tried to show the folly of this approach, but the beliefs are so prevalent in our culture that their voices are seldom heard. Even religious people who are free will advocates have been taken in by the determinism of the disease model simply because religion has been introduced in treatment through the Twelve Steps and AA model. For religious men and women, Twelve Steps has a very strong appeal because of its religious associations, but the conflicts with their own free will beliefs are often ignored as a result. George Vaillant (1983) notes this contradiction on the part of many religious people. He argues that AA simply converts people from one belief system to another. In the process, religious people are asked to abandon choice and behavior, which ought to be an essential component of their religion. Since the Bible calls drunkenness a sin and not a medical illness (1 Corinthians 6:10), perhaps Vaillant senses the obvious contradiction between the Twelve Steps theory and biblical teaching.

For those who believe, religion can be helpful in overcoming addiction. However, when extreme religious determinism is applied to addiction treatment, religion can actually become counterproductive. For those with this view of religion, one solution is not to form a treatment model based on deterministic theology. For those with a free will view of salvation and human behavior, biblical teaching can be used as an incentive for prevention and recovery, as Geisler (2001) points out, "From beginning to end the Bible affirms, both implicitly and explicitly, that human beings have free choice" (32).

The Religion of AA and Twelve Steps

Despite protestations to the contrary, the Twelve Steps theory and AA model of addiction treatment is religious in nature. It has roots in the deterministic theology of John Calvin, or what Norman Geisler would say is an extreme version of Calvinism. Most addiction specialists who write about the religion of AA do not understand the differing views in Protestant theology relative to free will and determinism. This controversy, however, mirrors the current controversy as to whether addiction is a disease or choice. Religious people also tend to be unaware of this issue. This means that religious people who believe in free will and choice as a matter of faith often become deterministic in their views of addiction because of the religious determinism of the Twelve Steps theory of addiction treatment.

People who are not religious are rightly offended at the Twelve Steps and AA model of treatment, and one cannot even summarize this treatment model without seeing the obvious religious overtones. Consider, for example, the way Miller (1998) summarizes the Twelve Steps treatment approach. Twelve Steps treatment involves: 1) turning one's will over to the Higher Power of your choice; 2) confessing the wrong things you have done; 3) making amends to others; 4) prayer and meditation; and 5) conforming oneself to the will of the Higher Power (984). Notice that this entire description is religious. In addition, the Twelve Steps model is a particular kind of religion that has a vaguely defined deity, a deterministic view of human nature, and a preference for the Big Book over the Bible.

For many, the most visible connection of religion to AA is the Oxford Group, which serves as the religious framework for the Twelve Steps theory. The real issue, however, is not religion or the peculiar beliefs of the Oxford Group, but a philosophy of determinism that is behind the religious connection. It is the bringing over of this aspect of religious thought that is detrimental to addiction treatment and not religion. For example, Kurtz (1979) analyzes the Five Procedures of the Oxford Group and suggests that the first (give in to God) is changed to "hopeless helplessness rather than salvation" (50). Kurtz suggests this is an attempt to avoid any religious association. Hopeless helplessness, however, is precisely the view of individual salvation in extreme Calvinism, so there actually has been no substitution but rather a shuffling of terminology with a misapplication to addiction treatment.

Sometimes concepts are attached to the language of the Bible without the Bible actually teaching the concept. Such is the case with what often happens in the Twelve Steps and AA treatment model. For example, Paul said, "You see, at just the right time, when we were still powerless, Christ died for the ungodly" (Romans 5:6). The NIV translates the Greek adjective *asthenes* as "powerless" while the New American Standard Bible (NASB) translates it "helpless." Both of these terms are often found in the literature of the Twelve Steps and AA model of addiction treatment and Romans 5:6 is often referenced by those who seek a biblical justification for this treatment approach. Although this terminology fits nicely with the argument that the addict is powerless and helpless in his addiction, it is actually a misapplication of the passage. Paul's subject in this text is salvation and not addiction, human behavior, or the ability to make choices. His argument is that humankind is powerless to provide a means of salvation, which is the point he makes two verses later in this chapter, "But God demonstrates his own love for us in this: While we were still sinners, Christ died for us" (v. 8).

Some might argue that terms like powerless and helplessness in this text can refer to a corrupt human nature and that humankind does not have the freedom to make good choices regarding behavior. A better interpretation of the text, however, is to understand that Paul is talking about humankind's helpless condition without Christ rather than the inability to choose to follow Christ. The idea is that we cannot save ourselves, or provide a meaningful sacrifice that would atone for our sins, but we can respond favorably to the good news of salvation, "For God so loved the world that he gave his one and only Son, that whoever believes in him shall not perish but have eternal life" (John 3:16). Although we cannot provide the means for this salvation, we can make the individual choice whether to accept it. Notice that the promise is for "whoever believes." This is in harmony with the open invitation of the gospel, "The

Spirit and the bride say, 'Come!'...and whoever wishes, let him take the free gift of the water of life" (Revelation 22:17).

Whether the subject is salvation, behavior, or addiction, the expectations of God for humankind is that freedom, free will, and choice are unique characteristics of the human race. The expectation is that people will freely come to God for salvation and guidance. Peter describes the longing of God for humankind to make the right choice in saying that God "is patient with you, not wanting anyone to perish, but everyone to come to repentance" (2 Peter 3:9). This verse demonstrates that every individual has the potential to make the right choice because God is described as "not wanting anyone to perish."

Knowing that God wants all to be saved does not relieve individuals of the responsibility of making the hard choices of discipleship, including counting the cost (Luke 14:28) and self-denial (Mark 8:34). Paul describes the Christian life as a race to the finish, and he encourages Christians to run "in such a way as to get the prize" (1 Corinthians 9:24) or "do not run like a man running aimlessly" (v. 26). He concludes by using himself as an example, "No, I beat my body and make it my slave so that after I have preached to others, I myself will not be disqualified for the prize" (v. 27). The analogy of the athlete indicates the need for individual discipline and choice relative to acceptable Christian behavior. These verses summarize biblical teaching relative to the struggle to control human behavior. When faced with compulsions to do things that have negative consequences, the easy way out is to say, "Please help me because I can't help myself!" Instead, the power is in each one to make the body a slave rather than being a slave of our compulsions.

There has been a marriage between the secular disease model view of addiction and the religious treatment model of Twelve Steps and AA. Both the disease model of addiction and the Twelve Steps and AA approach to treatment assume a view of human nature that suggests individuals cannot practice self-control because of some genetic or spiritual flaw. Regardless of what kind of religious belief one has, or whether one is secular or religious, everyone is better off adopting a treatment strategy based on a belief in free will and behavioral choice.

Jeffery Schaler (1996) notes the religious nature of AA by quoting directly from the Alcoholics Anonymous World Services (1976) Big Book, which is an official AA publication. The Big Book says, "He has commenced to accomplish those things for us which we could never do by ourselves" (25). This parallels the view of theological determinism that the sinner is unable to make any changes without a personal intervention by God. Rather than making an individual behavioral choice, the addict is urged to let the Big Book enable you "to find a Power greater than yourself which will solve your problem" (52).

So then, what should be done relative to the use of religion in addiction treatment? A pragmatic approach should be taken. If faith can make a positive contribution to treatment, then by all means it should be used, but a religious treatment model should never be forced on people who do not want it. Not only should friends and family avoid coercing people in religious treatment programs, but the government and courts have no business doing so either.

The purpose here is not to criticize Twelve Steps and AA for being religious, but for denying that it is religious, and also for not revealing that it is a certain kind of religion; that is, a religion that believes in a deterministic view of human behavior. Transparency is essential so that all people can find the best treatment program that fits their needs.

The Danger of Groupthink

A problem that exists in both religious and secular approaches to addiction treatment is the failure to distinguish the group from individual freedom to act. Although groups can be objectively and permanently defined, individuals can determine for themselves whether they want to be a part of the group. People move in and out of groups all the time. However, in both religion and addiction treatment, there are those who believe that individuals cannot choose to belong to or escape from various groups. Once a person is identified as belonging to a certain group, a pattern of self-deception can develop as the individual is forced to conform to the values and beliefs of the group. This behavior is sometimes called "groupthink" (Reber & Reber, 2001).

I recognized this behavior in a group therapy session I once observed. The group began with each member making some kind of opening statement such as, "My name is _____ and I am an alcoholic/drug addict." My first thought was, "Why are these people confessing to something they are not?" Members of this group were not currently engaging in alcohol or drug abuse because they were in prison. In addition, all of the group members expressed a commitment not to abuse alcohol and drugs in the future, yet everyone was encouraged to express these negative and self-defeating statements about themselves as if they were now what they had been in the past. In fact, if one of them had said, "I once abused alcohol but now I do not, and so now I am not an alcoholic," he would have been ridiculed by the group and accused of being in denial. The idea is that once a person has been labeled by others as being a part of a certain group, then he can never escape this identity. One would think this kind of labeling would be abhorrent to modern day thinking and in almost every other area it is. However, in addiction treatment the disease model prevails and people are constantly locked in groups. This is where the disease model of addiction is clearly harmful. It forces labels on people and does not encourage the power in each individual to decide whether he wants to continue in the group labeled "drug addict" or "alcoholic."

Who gets to label people? This is not something done as a result of scientific investigation, but is based on the subjective judgment of others as to whether people have lost control of their behaviors, and once labeled, people are said to be in denial if they attempt to reject the label. So, people are forced to conform to the beliefs of the group regarding their helpless conditions. The truth is, however, that people can and do move in and out of groups all the time. For example, a young man may go through a period of rebellion or experimentation where alcohol and drugs are abused. At the time, he may exhibit the out-of-control behavior that some label as a disease, but at a later time he may stop using drugs and alcohol completely or consume them on occasions in moderation. Yet, this person may still carry the label of alcoholic or drug addict the rest of his life. What is worse, the individual may start abusing alcohol or drugs again as a result of the false belief that he is helpless to do anything about controlling his behavior.

The idea of groupthink in addiction treatment has its background, if not its source, in theology. The argument of theological determinism is that an individual does not have a choice. In the same way, when someone is labeled as having the disease of addiction, the tendency is to behave like the label. If this belief is strong enough, then the individual loses faith in his ability to change his behavior.

Conclusion

The fatalistic view that all addicts have a disease can be countered with the view that all addicts have a choice. To say that addiction is a choice is heresy to the ears of many treatment specialists as well as the religion of the Twelve Steps. Addiction, however, is a behavior, and there is ample teaching in Scripture that suggests people choose their behaviors.

What we have learned in this chapter is that biblical religion, if taken seriously, can be both preventative and curative regarding addictive behavior. Unfortunately, some religious ideas have been misapplied to addiction treatment and this has prevented many from getting the help they need. The key to defeating addiction is understanding ourselves. We must recognize that there are no drugs or behaviors that we cannot choose to control, and biblical teaching suggests that we should engage in the struggle to control our bodily passions and compulsions. The good news is that by doing this we gain an increasing ability and maturity to govern our lives in ways that serve our own best interest.

Recommended Reading

For those interested in examining the free will perspective in Scripture, there is nothing better than Klein's (1990) *The New Chosen People: A Corporate View of Election.* If the book is no longer in print, search the internet for used copies. Norman Geisler (2001) argues against individual determinism in his book, *Chosen But Free.* He says that "moral obligations imply that we have self-determining moral free choice" and that *"ought* implies *can"* (30). His view is that John Calvin did not reject individual freedom and those who do so today practice a form of extreme Calvinism. For a discussion of the history and religious nature of AA, see Jeffrey Schaler's (2000) book, *Addiction is a Choice.* Schaler, like many treatment specialists who write about addiction, does not understand the influence of religious determinism on the Twelve Steps theory of addiction treatment, but he gives a good overall history and shows the connection of religion and the Oxford Group to the Twelve Steps theory and AA. Although Schaler is secular in his approach to addiction, I find very little that I would disagree with in his overall view of the subject. Mariana Valverde (1998) also gives an excellent historical survey of the religious origins of Twelve Steps and AA treatment model in her book *Diseases of the Will.* She also shows how Twelve Steps and AA have "successfully colonized many medical sites without having even the slightest medical credentials" (29). Her general argument is that addicts do not have a biological disease, but a diseased will. The "will's capacity for freedom can only be built up by freely exercising that very will, however diseased or out of shape it might be" (33).

Questions for Discussion

1. From your own experience, describe some of the ways people seek an Easy Button Religion and Easy Button Solutions to their problems. In what ways can this be harmful to people?

2. Addicts want the freedom to do drugs or engage in addictive behaviors. How is it that they can become enslaved by their addictions? Think about the ways the pursuit of freedom can turn to slavery.

3. What are psychosocial factors and why are they important in overcoming addiction?

4. What is the moral argument and when should it be used? For an addict who is religious and takes the Bible seriously, how can you use the moral argument in an effective way?

5. Discuss the issues in the debate over religious determinism and free will. How does all this affect addiction treatment for religious people?

6. Romans 5:6 says we are powerless. Look at the context of this verse carefully. In what way are we powerless? Does this mean we are powerless to control our behavior?

Chapter 4
Disease and Addiction

A Diseased View of Life

I saw a news report on television about a judge who released a man who had been found guilty of raping two children. Asked by some reporters why he let the sex offender go, the judge said that prison was not appropriate because this man has a disease. The basis for this outrageous decision was the judge's own belief in the disease model. It seems that the judge himself had an addiction to alcohol and had completely accepted the disease model of addiction. Concerning a convicted pedophile who had raped two children, the judge said: "He has a disease like I do." The truth is, neither the judge nor the convicted child rapist had a disease, and both of them were responsible for their own actions. Yet the judge used the disease model to rationalize his own behavior as well as excuse the behavior of a convicted pedophile. By blaming behavior on biology or genes, the judge relieves himself and others of the responsibility for their actions, and the logical consequence of his belief about his alcohol addiction is to extend the disease model to other behaviors. Sickness and genes, however, do not cause people to lose control of their behaviors, and addiction is not a disease. To accept the disease label implies that people must accommodate those who are sick by not holding them to account for their irresponsible behaviors, which in this case means that a convicted sex offender is released from prison.

Although the above example may seem extreme, it is the logical consequence of believing that behavior is the fault of biology. As Schaler (1998) notes, "The disease model is being applied to any socially unacceptable behavior as a means of absolving people of responsibility for their actions, criminal or otherwise" (236). When people feel absolved of responsibility for their actions, the expectations are that others must accommodate them in their sickness. As a society, we rightly make accommodations for people who are handicapped or disabled by attempting to remove the barriers that would prevent them from living life to the fullest extent possible. However, when this principle is applied to drug and alcohol abuse, gambling, shopping, eating, sex, and other behaviors, a perversion of this benevolent rule occurs. It exploits the goodness of society while crippling the will and confidence of those who are addicted.

The sickness label not only harms society, as the above illustration suggests, but it also harms those who are labeled. When people view strong desires and emotions as a sickness, they tend to display the behavior of whatever sickness they have been assigned; that is, they behave in all the ways suggested by the label. People feel helpless and hopeless about their condition and become passive participants in the treatment process. This means they look to doctors to cure them, or family to care for them, or employers to accommodate them, or religion to provide what they will not provide for themselves.

History of the Disease Model

The roots of the disease theory of addiction go all the way back to the late 1930's when the religious approach of AA was joined to the medical community's view of biological disease. This was a marriage of convenience since both groups held a deterministic view of their particular fields of interest; for example, the religious background of AA views salvation and human nature as preordained while medicine views disease as biological rather than psychological. The Center for Alcohol Studies and the National Council on Alcoholism were early advocates of the view that alcohol abuse is a disease. In 1956, their efforts led the American Medical Association to apply disease terminology to alcohol addiction (Rice, 1996). Through the influential work of men like Jellinek (1960) and Vaillant (1983), the disease model became the prevailing view, and in time, the sickness label spread to the abuse of other drugs and then to all kinds of problematic behaviors.

Eventually, these views began to encounter resistance from cognitive psychologists as well as specialists in the field of addiction treatment. The most influential attack on the disease model was by psychologist Stanton Peele (1989) in his book *Diseasing of America*. The work of Jeffery Schaler (1998, 2000) and Herbert Fingarette (1998) lend support to the arguments presented by Peele. These men and others began to develop different approaches to substance abuse treatment as an alternative to the usual AA involvement, the Twelve Steps theory, abstinence only, and permanent disease label.

Cognitive approaches often focus on the beliefs that people have about themselves and their environments. For example, if people are unhappy with the way they view themselves or their environments, they may turn to alcohol, drugs, gambling, or sex as a way to see themselves differently, or as a way to escape some difficult or unpleasant situation. The idea is to change people's beliefs about themselves and to help them understand why they choose addiction as a way to deal with life's issues. The focus is on changing thoughts and beliefs and, as Rian McMullin (2000) notes, "If we change our thoughts, we change ourselves" (6). Some cognitive approaches, like Motivational Interviewing (Miller & Rollnick, 2002), emphasize the advantages of change versus the disadvantages of the status quo. Most cognitive approaches help clients discover for themselves what it is that they value. This usually occurs in some type of appraisal process in which addicts assess the costs and benefits of continued drug and alcohol use.

Are You Bad or Sick?

A key component of the disease theory is the belief in loss of control of one's behavior. According to this theory, loss of control is an involuntary reaction to the presence of alcohol in the body. It is argued that when alcohol enters in the bloodstream, it produces an irresistible craving for more alcohol. This is said to be an involuntary biological reaction, similar to catching a cold or developing a fever. The sickness label implies that people do not choose to get sick, they are not bad because they are sick, and when they get sick, they need treatment. This concept is summarized in the often heard saying: "You're not bad, you're sick!" The disease label is not confined to alcohol, but expanded to include all kinds of behaviors. Today, people who have problems with gambling, sex, eating, shopping, smoking, or any other problematic behavior, can also claim the sickness label.

I counseled with a young man once about his alcohol abuse. He was labeled as an alcoholic by treatment professionals because he fit all the criteria. During rehab in a traditional disease model program, it had been pounded in his head that he had a disease and could never touch alcohol again without losing control. Instead of following their advice, he continued to abuse alcohol. His girlfriend encouraged him to come to me for counseling since nothing else seemed to work. At our first session, he began to tell me about his disease and loss of control. I pointed out that he did not have a disease and that he abused alcohol because that is what he wanted. This was the first time he had been told anything like this and he was shocked that I would say such a thing. As we continued our discussion of the negative consequences often associated with the disease view of addiction, he finally said: "Well, I really never did believe them when they said I had a disease anyway." His honest reflection on his previous treatment is the initial reaction of most people to the disease model. There is something about it that is illogical and counter intuitive, and yet this is what people are commonly told even to the point of intimidation and brainwashing. It seems that people are forced to accept what they intuitively know to be false!

A few weeks later in a counseling session, this young man confessed to me that he recently went out with some friends for dinner and consumed alcohol. I asked him, "Well, what happened? Did you go crazy? Did you go on another drinking binge?" He said, "No, I had the one drink and that was all." I asked, "What happened when you denied yourself another drink of alcohol? Did you run down the street screaming because you could not have another drink?" He smiled at this and said, "No, I did not have another drink because I did not want to get drunk. There are other things I want to do right now than drink all of the time." His response reveals a real danger in the disease model of addiction. The danger is that people who believe they cannot control their behavior continue to behave in keeping with the sickness label assigned to them by treatment professionals, family, and friends. As a result, the disease model establishes an addiction identity that makes it difficult for change to occur.

When I argue that it is legitimate to say people are bad rather than sick when they abuse alcohol, I am not making a moralistic judgment of personal condemnation. From a biblical standpoint, Jesus warned against judging people, "Do not judge, or you too will be judged. For in the same way you judge others, you will be judged, and with the measure you use, it will be measured to you" (Matthew 7:1-2). But in the same chapter, Jesus encouraged people to make righteous judgments regarding people's behavior, "By their fruit you will recognize them" (v. 16). So, there is a difference between judging or attacking the person and judging a behavior. According to biblical teaching, drunkenness is a behavior that excludes one from the kingdom of God (1 Corinthians 6:10). For those who take the Bible seriously, this ought to provide a great incentive to change behavior. Those who do not accept biblical morality still recognize that some behaviors are bad in the sense that they are harmful to themselves and others. The goal is not to personally condemn people simply because they hold to unconventional values, but to help them recognize when a behavior is harmful and irresponsible. If people refuse to recognize the harm they bring to themselves and others, and if they continue to prefer the immediate gratification of alcohol abuse over the long-term benefits of either abstaining or controlling their drinking, then there is not much that can be done.

Behavior is Not Biology

It is important that we distinguish a disease from a behavior. People *have* diseases but they *do* behaviors. Some behaviors are very destructive to the human body, and they can aggravate or bring about certain diseases. However, we should never confuse a behavior with a disease, or the cause of a disease with the disease itself. If people drink large amounts of alcohol over a long period of time they damage their internal organs and likely develop heart disease or cirrhosis of the liver. Drinking alcohol is a behavior and not the disease it may cause. Diet and lifestyle choices can make us more susceptible to disease, but diet and lifestyle are choices, while diabetes and cancer are diseases. Drugs affect the body in different ways and the severity of the reaction often depends on the individual. Putting drugs in one's body, however, is not a disease but a choice. In contrast to a behavior, a disease is involuntary; that is, I cannot choose whether I have an epileptic seizure, or diverticulosis, but I can choose whether to drink alcohol, use cocaine, or smoke cigarettes. If a real disease is biological, and it is, then it does not do any good to try and talk to it, or feel guilty about it, or wish it away; instead, it must be treated medically. Behavior, however, is not biology, and the key to clarifying the whole issue is to separate the two. To illustrate, drinking alcohol and smoking cigarettes are behaviors, cirrhosis of the liver and lung cancer are diseases.

To say that people have no control over their choices is to deny a fundamental aspect of their God-given humanness. Humankind was created in the image of God (Genesis 1:27), which implies that Adam and Eve had the capacity to make a choice regarding their behavior. God commanded the man, "You are free to eat from any tree in the garden; but you must not eat from the tree of the knowledge of good and evil, for when you eat of it you will surely die" (Genesis 2:16-17). The statement, "You are free to eat," suggests that people are free to make choices. The behavior of Adam and Eve was not the result of their chemicals, genes, or brainwaves but the result of their own choices; yet, many argue that this is not possible when it comes to addiction. Notice that God said, "You are free to eat...but you must not eat." In contrast, many argue that before we can be free, we must first admit that we are not free because of a disease and that we cannot control our behavior.

Medical doctors have become experts at tracing the progression of damage done by alcohol to the human body, but this does not explain why a person would want to consume large amounts of alcohol (Schaler, 1997, 2000). People use drugs and alcohol for various psychological and emotional reasons and not because they have some kind of allergy to alcohol that produces involuntary behavior. The argument is often made that some people are genetically predisposed to consume alcohol, but even if this is the case, there is no evidence to suggest that this causes people to lose control. Behaviors are not inherited and they are not caused by genes. An important goal in addiction treatment should be to discover the reason why people choose certain behaviors. In diseases one should look for the cause, but in behaviors one should look for the reason. People tend to behave in certain ways based on how they view themselves. For a variety of reasons, people make choices based on what they value at the moment. In contrast, the idea that people cannot control their behaviors is a belief that is held with religious fervor by disease model proponents. Those who question this theory are often dismissed as being unscientific and ignorant of the plain facts. Yet, abundant evidence has existed for more than 30 years that contradicts the loss of control theory and these studies are frequently cited in the non-disease literature. For example, Jeffrey Schaler (2000) summarizes several experiments that show that problem drinkers can moderate their drinking if given the right incentives. When the incentives are withdrawn, problem drinkers return to their regular patterns of excessive drinking (22-25), which clearly demonstrates that there is no such thing as an irresistible craving or loss of control. These studies have either been ignored or rejected by disease model proponents.

The Sobells (1993) argue against the necessity of total abstinence and show that it is possible for those who are problem drinkers to control their drinking without the usual expectation of worsening symptoms. According to the authors, controlled drinking is the development of certain cognitive skills and techniques that teach individuals how to control their drinking to a point where it is no longer a problem. The Sobells argue that a "sizable proportion of individuals with alcohol problems can solve their problems on their own if they are sufficiently motivated and are provided with some guidance and support" (xi). What this shows is that people retain control over their own behavior. The key to change, however, is motivation, which is the reason that not all those with alcohol problems change.

Help Me Because I Can't Help Myself!

A consequence of believing that people cannot control their behavior is that they are also entitled to special treatment because they are sick. This belief has now become so ingrained in the fabric of our society and culture that it is seldom questioned. Yet, the common sense thinking of most people tends to resist this line of reasoning. Most seem to have an intuitive recognition that this is just an excuse for irresponsible behavior.

I once listened to a conversation among several school teachers regarding the alcohol policy at the school where they taught. It seems that teachers could show up at school drunk as long as they reported their situation to the principal. As long as they reported their drunken condition, they would receive paid time off as well as free treatment. As the teachers discussed this among themselves, they viewed the policy as one that rewarded irresponsible behaviors and they jokingly suggested to one another that they should all show up at school drunk so they also could get some paid time off. The school policy suggests the drunkard has no control over his drinking, but the teachers sensed he did and the paid time off was an abuse of sick leave. So, why would the school district tolerate such a nonsensical policy? Because they have been told by many in the medical community that the alcohol abuser has a disease, which implies some kind of innocence regarding bad behavior. The attitude of the above group of teachers illustrates the ambivalence in the minds of the general public regarding the disease model of addiction. After more than fifty years of promotion, a large majority of the public now accepts the disease model of addiction, but their common sense tells them that people drink because they want to (Raul Caetano, 1987).

The disease model, AA, and the Twelve Steps treatment theory "medicalize substance abuse in such a way as to alleviate personal responsibility and related guilt" (Grandfield & Cloud, 1996, 47). This gives the drug abuser the authority to say, "Do not accuse me of acting irresponsibly, just accommodate me in my sickness." Or, as in the above story of the drunk teacher, "If I show up at work drunk, you cannot fire me, just give me some time off and pay for my treatment." Another example can be found in the GamAnon 1991 One Day Conference Book under the heading, "The Compulsive Gambler Speaks to His Family." In this example, family members are rebuked if they blame gambling addicts for their behavior, "You wouldn't treat me that way for having leukemia or diabetes. Compulsive gambling is a disease, too."

In July, 2006, Mel Gibson was charged by the police with driving under the influence of alcohol and going 40 miles per hour over the posted speed limit. At his arrest, he cursed the arresting officer as well as made outrageous statements regarding a certain ethnic group. Gibson issued a statement of apology that appeared in the media. In his statement, he appealed to the sickness label to explain his behavior, which suggests that he did not believe he was fully responsible for his actions. For example, if I have the flu, I should not be expected to perform my job, family, and relationship responsibilities as effectively as if I were well. Likewise, if Gibson has a relapse of his alcoholism disease, then people are supposed to make certain allowances for his behavior.

Mel Gibson did not drive while drunk because he was sick. His conduct is the result of a pattern of behavior he began many years before. It is likely due to his own dysfunctional approach to dealing with problems of daily living, or some unhappiness in how he views himself or his environment. Considering his wealth and fame as an actor, few can sympathize with his meager issues while they have far greater burdens to bear. Would Gibson have acted this way had he been sober? Probably not, but he knew exactly what he was doing when he ingested large amounts of alcohol. This man is intelligent and knows all about how alcohol can lower his inhibitions as well as affect his mental state. At no point in this process did someone put a gun to his head and force him to consume alcohol. He was not forced to behave irresponsibly and he could have stopped at any point along the way. Even while under the influence of the drug, he still could have made better decisions about his behavior. Although alcohol may lower inhibitions and provide feelings of euphoria and empowerment, it does not force people to do things. The desire for food and sex can be strong as well, but they can also be controlled.

In February, 2005, a little girl named Jessica Lunsford was kidnapped, raped, and murdered by a pedophile and convicted sex offender named John Couey. One night I happened to hear portions of his taped confession on a news channel. Interspersed in his confession were his statements saying, "I'm sick" and "I have a terrible disease." The news reports revealed all the sordid details of this sex offender's life. His life was aimless and without purpose. He was often in jail because of theft of property or a sex offense. It seems that he was never willing to hold himself accountable for his actions, and his belief that he was not bad but sick was reinforced by the medical community. As far back as 1978, Couey wrote to his attorney that his doctors told him that he behaved the way he did because he had a disease. John Couey did not have a disease, he had a behavior problem. He was a thief because he thought it was easier to steal than to work, and he was a child molester because he refused to control inappropriate sexual desires. His use of alcohol and cocaine silenced whatever conscience he had and gave him the courage to act on his impulses.

Someone pointed out to me once that a pedophile's brainwaves are different, as if this proves they are sick rather than bad, or somehow not responsible for their actions, but this proves nothing. Brainwaves and genes do not force people to do anything. Even if it can be proven that there is some genetic difference or unusual brain activity among those who are pedophiles, this does not mean that they are not responsible for their actions. All of us have different personalities and experiences in life, and although these conditions may influence the decisions we make, they do not force us to behave badly.

Alcoholism Defined

I prefer not to use the term "alcoholic" or "alcoholism" because I do not agree with the way these terms are commonly defined. Implied in the definition of alcoholism is a denial of an important aspect of our humanness, which is the ability to make choices. For those who believe the Bible, the idea that humans are sick rather than bad should be rejected as contrary to Scripture. Adam and Eve were not driven from the garden because they were sick but because they were bad. The story of the Bible reveals the choices that people make and how this affects their lives on earth, their relationship with God, and eventually their eternal destiny. The prophet Ezekiel rejected the notion that we can blame something or someone else for our behavior, "The soul who sins is the one who will die" (Ezekiel 18:20).

There is now a growing consensus in the mental health field that people can actually choose their behavior and that they are not controlled by their genes or environment. Many psychologists now argue that there are no predetermined and automatic responses to life events and the focus ought to be on how to change behavior by thinking differently. I am also in agreement with this new direction in psychology, and what cognitive psychologists now say about behavior, choice, and self-control is in general agreement with biblical teaching.

To see how the cognitive approach to mental health and behavior contrasts with the disease model of addiction, we must first define alcoholism according to the standard definition. Although there may be some variants to the disease model, they all have common themes. The definition used here is from the website of the National Council on Alcoholism and Drug Dependence (1990). The definition was approved by the Boards of Directors of the National Council on Alcoholism and Drug Dependence, Inc. and the American Society of Addiction Medicine in February of 1990.

> Alcoholism is a primary, chronic disease with genetic, psychosocial, and environmental factors influencing its development and manifestations. The disease is often progressive and fatal. It is characterized by continuous or periodic: impaired control over drinking, preoccupation with the drug alcohol, use of alcohol despite adverse consequences, and distortions in thinking, most notably denial. (1)

The disease component of this definition is later defined as "an involuntary disability." Impaired control is further defined as "the inability to limit alcohol use or to consistently limit on any drinking occasion the duration of the episode, the quantity consumed, and/or the behavioral consequences of drinking." Notice that the characterization of this disease is not described in terms of biology but behavior. No biology is mentioned in the definition, but a true disease would be described in biological rather than behavioral terms. Furthermore, there is no blood test or physical examination that can determine whether people will not control their behavior. Doctors may become experts about what alcohol does to the body after it is consumed, but this is not an explanation of the cause of the behavior.

A Real Disease

I once had a doctor examine my colon for signs of cancer. Thankfully, he found no cancer, but he did discover that I had diverticulosis, which is a condition where tiny pockets, called diverticula, develop along the wall of the large intestine. If something is lodged in one of these pockets, it is possible for an infection and inflammation to occur. Diverticulitis can be very painful, and in some cases it can require the surgical removal of part of the intestine. About one third of people over the age of 50 have diverticulosis, but most people have no symptoms of diverticular disease and only find out they have it when they have a colonoscopy. There is no cure for this disease, but doctors believe a high fiber diet is beneficial and may prevent more diverticula from forming as well as lessen the chance of an attack of diverticulitis.

Notice how the description of this disease is totally different from the discussions regarding alcoholism. Go to any medical website for information on diverticulosis and the discussion focuses on biology rather than behavior, but in the discussions of alcoholism, the focus is on behavior and not biology. The same is true for all other so-called diseases of behavior, like gambling, shopping, sexual activity, and so forth.

Someone might respond by saying that I am being asked to manage diverticular disease with a high fiber diet just as the alcoholic is asked to manage his alcoholism disease by total abstinence, the Twelve Steps theory, and AA meetings. This, however, is a good example of comparing apples with oranges. Diverticula disease is biological and can be observed by a physician. I did not choose this disease and the disease itself is not a behavior, but consuming large quantities of alcohol over a long period of time is a behavior. In my case, the doctor did not try to find some out-of-control behavior in my life and identify it as diverticulosis. He did not say, "You have an allergy to low fiber foods that cause you to lose control of your behavior. You must never eat low fiber foods again because this disease makes these foods irresistible." Instead, he focused on biology, and showed me the pictures of my disease. In this way, the fallacy of the alcohol disease issue can now be clearly defined: a behavior is not a disease.

It is argued that gambling is also a disease, but a doctor cannot examine a person's body and discover any evidence that it is a disease. There is no blood test or physical observation that suggests one cannot control gambling. A physical exam might show the results of gambling. For example, if a person gambles away all of his money, he may be malnourished because he cannot buy food, but this condition could just as easily be the result of some other kind of behavior. The doctor may say: "You must now manage your gambling disease by not gambling, attending Gamblers Anonymous (GA) for the rest of your life, and accepting the Twelve Steps theory." But how does the doctor know whether the disease is gambling or shopping since both can cause one to become impoverished? Likewise, uncontrolled sexual activity may cause one to develop a sexually transmitted disease (STD), but an STD is a true disease while sexual activity is a behavior. Although the distinction between behavior and disease appears obvious, it is usually dismissed in the discussion of alcohol abuse. George Vaillant (1983), for example, argues that the defining characteristic of alcoholism is when "an individual has lost capacity consistently to control how much and how often he drinks..." (17). Drinking large amounts of alcohol can affect human biology and this can be observed by a physician, but drinking alcohol is a behavior while cirrhosis of the liver is a disease.

Disease and Denial

I was amazed at the enthusiasm of the doctor as he showed me the video of the inside of my colon, but I did not share his enthusiasm. I thought to myself, "I don't want to see this!" Nevertheless, he said enthusiastically, "You've got a bad case of diverticulosis! Just look at these pockets along your intestinal wall! Look here, and look over here!" Well, there is no denying it, that is my colon and those are my diverticula. So, when the doctor suggested a high fiber diet for the prevention of diverticulitis, I agreed to change my eating habits. For me to argue otherwise is to be in denial about my physical condition.

Ted and Sue were happily married. Ted always kept a few beers in the refrigerator for himself and his friends when they would come over. Sue abstained from alcohol and never liked keeping alcohol in the house. On one occasion, Ted had too much to drink and was stopped by the police and charged with DUI. Sue was upset over this, and talked with her minister the next day at church. The preacher, who accepted the disease model of addiction, told Sue that he thought her husband was sick with the terrible disease of alcoholism. He suggested that they meet the next day with representatives of the local drug and alcohol rehab center. Professionals at the rehab center confirmed to Sue that Ted was sick and that this disease would get progressively worse unless Sue put Ted into their expensive 28 day alcohol treatment program. So, one day when Ted arrived home from work, he was confronted by his wife, the minister, and several treatment specialists who insisted that Ted go immediately into drug treatment. When Ted laughed at the notion that he was sick, they all said, "Ted, you are in denial!"

Notice how different these stories are relative to denial. In the first story, the diagnosis is based on objective, observable, biological data about a physical condition. The second story is based on subjective interpretations of behavior. In this case, the charge of denial can become a form of brainwashing and intimidation used by a group to convince an individual to enter some kind of rehabilitation or AA program.

Some people do not want help and they do not wish to change their behavior. In providing help, the goal should be to convince people that it is in their own best interest to discontinue a habit that causes negative consequences. If people are not ready for change, they should not be forced in treatment for engaging in behavior that others may view as self-destructive. In the example of Ted, he may not have been in denial at all about his condition. He had acted irresponsibly and had gotten a DUI conviction and this may be enough to cause him to reassess his drinking and behavior patterns. To charge him with denial simply because he does not accept the sickness label is going too far.

Denial is real, and it is a characteristic of the human condition, but it should not be thought of as something primarily associated with drug and alcohol abuse. Denial is a part of deception, and the tendency is to be deceived about many aspects of our lives. The first sin recorded in the Bible involved the deception of Eve. Regarding the tree of the knowledge of good and evil, God said, "you must not eat" and "when you eat of it you will surely die" (Genesis 2:17). When Eve repeated this command to the serpent (3:3), the serpent said, "You will not surely die" (v. 4). In 1 Timothy 2:14, Paul said she had been deceived about the matter. Ever since that time, humankind has been deceived about one thing or another.

The Bible tells the story of King Saul's failure to carry out the instructions of God concerning a group of people called the Amalekites. This sin was so serious that it cost Saul his kingship. When confronted by the prophet Samuel about his flagrant disobedience to God, Saul denied it, "But I did obey the Lord" (1 Samuel 15:20). How can an act of disobedience that is so obvious in the story be denied by the one who did it? The answer is that humankind has the capacity to deny the obvious.

In addiction, the biggest deception is the belief that people can evade the consequences of their actions, but the Bible warns, "Do not be deceived: God cannot be mocked. A man reaps what he sows" (Galatians 6:7). There is no doubt that the deeper one goes in addiction the harder it will be to come out. One of the greatest obstacles to recovery is deception about the reality of one's condition. One should not minimize the difficulty of being in the depths of addiction, but this condition is the end of a long process of decision-making. When people first start down this path they are more clearheaded than when they finish. There is testimony in Scripture to suggest that our past decisions can cause us to be deceived. The Bible talks about the "evil that deceives those who are perishing" (2 Thessalonians 2:10). What, then, can people do who have followed the path of deception and denial regarding addiction? Perhaps, the only chance is for them to have some kind of dramatic awakening about their condition similar to what is described in Miller and C'de Baca (2001).

Drugs Do Not Cause Addiction

The National Rifle Association (NRA) has a popular saying, "Guns don't kill people, people kill people." They like to put this saying on bumper stickers so that people are reminded about a fundamental difference between guns and the people who use them to harm others.

Gun control advocates do not like this saying because it takes away from the legitimacy of what they want to do, which is to remove guns from society. Gun opponents believe that the more guns that are removed from society the less violence there will be. The NRA makes the following reply, "If guns are outlawed, then only outlaws will have guns." Setting aside for a moment the issue of whether we ought to force people to give up their guns, notice how similar the argument is to the present discussion. Gun control advocates see the guns as the source of violence while the NRA sees bad behavior as the source. Although I am not a big fan of guns, I must admit that the NRA has the more sensible argument. Killing people is a behavior. While guns are neither good nor evil, people can use them in evil and irresponsible ways. On the other hand, no one would deny the legitimate use of guns by police and military, and few would deny the use of guns for hunting and self-protection. So, the argument of gun opponents tends to focus on the guns rather than the behavior. The idea is that if we can just get rid of guns we can stop violence. This assumes, of course, that people will not resort to other methods of hurting one another.

In a similar way, discussions concerning addiction tend to focus on the object of the addiction rather than the behavior. If the addiction involves drugs, then an assumption is often made that drugs have the power to force people to consume them. This seems to be the position our society has taken toward drugs; that is, we have a war on drugs rather than on behavior. Further evidence of this is the banning and criminalization of certain drugs in society. To focus on the legality, availability, and chemical properties of drugs avoids addressing the importance of behavior and the reasons why people choose to use drugs. To focus on drugs instead of behavior can give the impression that people cannot control their behavior, which is a hindrance to recovery. Drugs do not cause addiction, people cause addiction. Neither the legalization nor criminalization of drugs prevents certain people from following the path of drug addiction. If certain drugs are not available, they find substitutes, or engage in addictive behaviors that do not involve drugs.

Video poker is said to be the most addictive slot machine game in casinos. This game is supposed to have mysterious powers that cause some people to lose control of their gambling. Video poker, however, is neither good nor evil—it is only a game, and if this game were banned, these people would find some other game to play. Video poker has no special powers and it does not cause addiction. Addiction is a behavior and video poker is a game of chance. Others explain this behavior by arguing that people who lose a lot of money playing video poker must be sick with a so-called gambling disease. It is argued that this game takes advantage of a genetic or mental defect that prevents some people from controlling their behavior. Even if it can be shown that the brainwaves of those who enjoy gambling are different from the brainwaves of those who do not, this does not prove that a game causes involuntary behavior in people. Instead, people gamble and play games because they find it pleasurable. For a variety of reasons, some people choose the immediate gratification of gambling despite the long-term negative consequences that this activity can bring. But why would someone do something that is so damaging in the long-term? The answer would be similar to that given for other self-destructive behaviors in which people engage. Perhaps they choose not to think about it, or they engage in self-deception about what they are doing. They may seek a way to escape their current unpleasant environment, or they seek to change the way they view themselves, or all of the above.

I once counseled with a man who was grossly overweight. He could walk only a few steps and required a wheelchair for mobility. His weight caused or aggravated many serious health problems, including diabetes. I tried to help him see that it would be in his own interest to lose some weight, but he rejected this option. He argued, "It is impossible for me to lose weight. You see, I have a terrible disease and I cannot control my eating." He was convinced he was completely helpless in the matter, and so he accepted the fact that he would continue to have ill health and die an early death. This attitude was unfortunate because there was much that he could have done to lose weight and improve the quality and longevity of his life. However, because this man believed he had a disease, he had given up on improving his condition. A better response would have been, "I have a terrible disease called diabetes and I must find a way to control my eating habits so that I can better manage this disease."

Some would argue that his unsuccessful efforts to control his eating was a disease since it is related to his diabetes. Others point out that this parallels the disease of alcoholism in that it contributes to cirrhosis of the liver and heart disease. It is true that chronic disease can be caused by many factors, including lifestyle choices. Make sure, however, that you do not confuse the cause of a disease with the disease itself. For some people, adult diabetes may be caused by eating habits or being overweight, but overeating is not a disease. Cirrhosis of the liver may be caused by drinking large amounts of alcohol over a long period of time, but drinking alcohol is a behavior and not a disease. Lung cancer can often be attributed to smoking cigarettes over many years, but smoking cigarettes is a behavior and not a disease.

Conclusion

A contradictory belief, held with religious fervor by many who believe in the sickness label of addiction, is that you cannot be free of addiction unless you are first willing to admit that you are helpless. This belief is in conflict with both experiments in human behavior and biblical teaching. People are encouraged to believe that a disease, genes, or brainwaves makes them act irresponsibly. Although genes are a defining element of our physiological makeup, they do not determine whether, or to what extent, people will take drugs, overeat, gamble, or practice some other self-destructive behavior. Instead of dealing with the issues of life, some people choose the immediate gratification of drugs, alcohol, gambling, shopping, and other behaviors. Applying the sickness label to those who choose to take drugs, gamble, or overeat is unfair and cruel to those who really are sick with a biological disease. People who battle real diseases have little in common with those who choose not to control their behavior. Finally, the disease label should be rejected because it is an obstacle to recovery. Peele (1989) notes, "People's belief that they have a disease makes it less likely that they will outgrow the problem" (27).

Recommended Reading

If I had only one book to read on this subject, it would be *Addiction is a Choice* by Jeffrey Schaler (2000). This book is concise, to the point, and very readable. Also check out

his chapter titled "Drugs and Free Will" (1998) in *Drugs: Should we Legalize, Decriminalize or Deregulate?* In my opinion, Schaler does the best job of explaining the difference between a real disease and a behavior. Refer to his website, which is filled with helpful links to his other writings and debates (http://www.schaler.net/index.html). *Diseasing of America* by Stanton Peele (1989) is the foundational work in this area and this book has much to offer in helping us understand the disease mindset in our culture. Finally, the book, *Heavy Drinking,* by Herbert Fingarette (1998) also deserves mention as an excellent refutation of the disease model approach to addiction.

Questions for Discussion

1. There is a story in this chapter about a judge who would not send a convicted pedophile to prison because he said he has a disease just like alcoholics. In this instance, how has the disease model impacted criminal justice in the United States?
2. What are some of the damaging effects of the sickness label on those who believe their behavior is the result of a disease?
3. Discuss the saying, "You're not bad, you're sick." This is usually applied to alcohol addiction, but can you think of some other areas of behavior where this statement might be problematic? What does it sound like when this saying is used in the context of criminal behavior?
4. If poor diet and eating habits can lead to or aggravate the disease of diabetes, why is it unreasonable to think that drinking alcohol might lead to the disease of alcoholism? (Remember, do not confuse the cause of a disease with the disease itself.)
5. How is the disease of diverticulosis different from the disease of alcoholism or gambling?
6. Is denial real? How does denial operate in addiction as well as other aspects of our lives? Discuss some biblical examples of denial.
7. How is the NRA slogan, "Guns don't kill people, people kill people," relevant to discussions about addiction? Do drugs cause addiction?

Chapter 5
The ABCs of Addiction

Thinking and Doing

A psychologist at the prison where I did some volunteer counseling recommended that I read a book in preparation for my work with prison inmates. The book by Robert Hare (1993) titled, *Without Conscience: The Disturbing World of the Psychopaths Among Us*, is about people with little or no conscience. This book was supposed to prepare me for many of the people I would be working with in prison. Hare tells the story of convicted murderer Gary Gilmore who was executed in 1977. In an interview, Gilmore was asked why he killed two people: "I wasn't thinkin', I wasn't plannin', I was just doin.'" He said later about the murders: "I'm just saying that murder vents rage. Rage is not reason. The murders were without reason" (58).

Gilmore's belief about why he did things is typical of those who behave in harmful and self-destructive ways. Psychopaths live day-to-day without regard for the future or the negative consequences of their actions. This kind of thinking is also characteristic of many people who give themselves over to addiction. I once counseled with a woman about her addiction who told me, "I do drugs for the same reason I do sex—I like it." My goal in counseling was to help her see that it was not in her own best interest to continue her drug habit. At the time, her behavior had brought her poor health, poverty, misery, and prison, but she made no connection between her behavior and her condition. This woman did not like her miserable condition, but she was proud that she never bothered with thinking and planning. Her focus was on doing rather than thinking.

I have also worked with people who understand that their behavior is harmful, but they have no idea why they continue to behave the way they do. I counseled with a young lady in her early twenties who had been in and out of jail all her young life. It seems that once she was around certain people she would behave in self-destructive ways. She was puzzled about this and was wondering if perhaps her behavior was some kind of automatic response to being around her friends. Her opening statement to me was, "I want to know why I do what I do because I am tired of going to jail." Her question is the key to solving her problems, and this question is a significant first step toward a solution. Her problem is that she does not recognize that it is her belief about herself and her friends and not her friends that is causing her problems. She falsely believed she was just doing and not thinking, but in this instance, her behavior was connected to her belief about herself. Until she learns to view herself differently, she will continue to behave in harmful ways when she is around certain people. She will continue to have problems until she recognizes that her beliefs are connected to her problems.

In the above examples, there are two major flaws taking place concerning behavior. First, all of the individuals were operating their lives under the mistaken belief that behavior is an automatic response to the events of life. They believe they are helpless to control their behavior because they think it occurs automatically, but the truth is, there are no automatic or predetermined responses to life events. Notice how this contrasts with present day beliefs about addiction. When people get around alcohol and drugs, or walk into a casino, or see pornography, they believe they suddenly start behaving automatically to their environment. For example, Bob was a man I worked with who came to me because he was discouraged that he had recently gambled away his paycheck at a local casino in Las Vegas. It seems that he just happened to go in a casino right after he got paid and two hours later he was broke. Bob said, "I can't explain it, something just happened when I walked into that casino, and by the time I realized what was happening, I was broke." According to him, he was doing rather than thinking, but is this really true? Actually, his behavior was based on a long history of decision-making over many years. These decisions were choices he made based on certain beliefs at the time, and over the years the behavior that seemed to him to be automatic was really based on his prior beliefs about himself and his environment. Gambling was a way for Bob to escape some of the disappointments he had with his life as well as give him hope that he could find an easy way to become rich and important. The few times he did win reinforced his dream of becoming rich but he always lost his winnings and more as he continued to gamble. Instead of finding a more realistic way of building his self-esteem, he longed for a quick and easy way through gambling. Bob's faulty thinking allowed him to fall victim to the myth that if you just gamble enough, you will win. The reality is that if you gamble at the slot machines long enough you will *always* lose everything. In other words, if you win ten million dollars on your first play, you will lose it all back if you continue to gamble. In addition, if you play long enough you win, but you will never win as much as you lose. The good feeling people get when they occasionally win keeps them playing.

The second flaw in thinking in the above examples is the lack of spiritual insight (see chapter 2). These individuals have a very worldly focus that prevents them from standing outside of themselves and viewing things differently. The focus is on immediate gratification without any consideration of future benefits or negative consequences. Never once do these individuals ask, "Is this really in my own best interest?" or "Will this help me reach my future goals of happiness?" Gilmore kills out of rage and Bob gambles to be somebody, but Gilmore does not think about why he is angry and Bob does not consider more realistic ways of building up his self-esteem; instead, both believe they are just doing and not thinking.

People falsely believe they cannot control their behavior because their focus is on the immediate gratification of doing. The more they live like this, the harder it is to see anything outside of the immediate context of their behavior. Concerning people like this, the Bible says, "Having lost all sensitivity, they have given themselves over to sensuality so as to indulge in every kind of impurity, with a continual lust for more" (Ephesians 4:19).

The ABC Model

To understand the ABCs of addiction, it is important that we understand something about psychology as well as biblical teaching. A brief discussion of cognitive restructuring helps us understand why there is no such thing as doing without thinking. The word cognitive has to do with rationality and thinking, and restructuring has to do with the process of changing faulty thinking. As psychologist Rian McMullin (2000) says, "If we change our thoughts, we change ourselves" (6). I like the idea changing our thoughts because it sounds a lot like biblical teaching. Jesus, for example, noted that evil thoughts precedes evil behavior, "For out of the heart come evil thoughts, murder, adultery, sexual immorality, theft, false testimony, slander" (Matthew 15:19). Perhaps this is why I had an intuitive connection to cognitive restructuring in my training as a counselor. I must admit, when I first started preaching, my focus was more on behavior rather than thinking. I would often say, "Do this, but don't do this!" In the practical application of the gospel, I remember telling people, "If you start doing better, then you start feeling better." There is certainly truth in this, and Paul noted the significant behavior change among the brothers at Corinth. After listing behaviors that were not compatible with the Christian life, he said: "And that is what some of you were" (1 Corinthians 6:11), which suggests they were able and willing to make significant changes in their behavior. Changing behavior, however, is really not the hard part. The hard part is changing the thinking that precedes the behavior, as Jesus says, "For out of the heart come evil thoughts..." So, my preaching now tends to focus on what takes place in the heart, or mind of the hearer, rather than the outward behavior. The idea is to work from the inside out and the behavior flows from the heart.

In Scripture, the heart represents the seat of emotions as well as the beliefs and thinking of the individual. For example, Paul warns Christians regarding a false belief by commanding, "Do not say in your heart..." (Romans 10:6). Their hearts represented their way of thinking or belief on a given point. The lesson here is that we can be more successful in changing behavior if we first change the heart or beliefs. To me, one of the most practical illustrations of this in Scripture is Peter's command to "prepare your minds for action" (1 Peter 1:13).

In the field of mental health, there has been a gradual evolution over time in thinking and practice. In the 1950s, B. F. Skinner developed principles that were able to predict and modify behavior patterns. Later, people like Albert Ellis, Aaron Beck, and Donald Meichenbaum noted the connection of beliefs to behavior. This approach became known as cognitive-behavior therapy. Today, the emphasis on thinking and beliefs is so strong that it is usually called cognitive therapy.

The best illustration of the cognitive approach to mental health is the ABC model. This model shows people that their beliefs are connected to their problems, which in addiction is crucial. For example, it is not drugs, but the beliefs about drugs that cause people problems. Instead of focusing on their beliefs, however, many people tend to blame biology, genetics, parents, childhood experiences, and bad luck for their addictions. They tend to blame their behaviors on everything but their own faulty thinking.

The ABC model is an acronym that stands for the three critical elements of how we respond to our environment. The A stands for some activating event or action that we experience in our environment. The A can represent a situation we happen to find ourselves in or a stimulus or trigger from our environment. For example, in the above story of Bob, the A represents the occasion when he went in a casino, which started off the whole process of his reacting in the way that he did. The C stands for the consequence of A; that is, it is the behavior that results from A. The C, or consequence of A, can be a feeling, like a depressed mood, anxiety, fear, or anger, or it can be a behavior like gambling or drug abuse. In Bob's case, the C was gambling away his paycheck. Most of the local casinos in Las Vegas offer a free check cashing service because people often behave like Bob. The casinos do this to create an ideal A event by getting people like Bob in the casino and then providing them with money.

Bob falsely believes that A produces C; that is, by going into the casino with money he automatically responds by gambling away his money. Actually, there are no A $\rightarrow$ C kinds of responses; instead, there will always be a B between the A and the C. The B stands for the beliefs we have about A. It is not so much the negative events of our lives that cause us problems but what we believe about those events. So, the correct formula is: A $\rightarrow$ B $\rightarrow$ C. When we respond inappropriately to life events it is because we have formulated a belief about a situation that is not true. As easy as the ABC model sounds, it is a difficult concept for people to grasp and put in practice. I teach a beginning counseling course at University of Nevada, Las Vegas (UNLV) and I spend a great deal of time on the ABC formula. On tests, however, many of the students argue that anger is an automatic response, as in "You make me angry!" People do not make us angry, it is what we believe about people that makes us angry. Gary Gilmore's belief that "rage is not reason" is false because there is a belief that is behind all anger.

Anger may be a response based on what we correctly believe about people, but it can also be a response based on faulty thinking. For example, Bob invites his wife, Sue, to dinner on Friday evening after both get off from work. Their plans are to go to the restaurant together at 6:00 PM when Bob arrives home from work, but at 6:45 Bob has not arrived. How will Sue respond? There are many possibilities, but they all depend on what Sue believes about why Bob is late. If Sue believes he is out gambling again, she will likely be angry or disappointed. If she believes he has had an accident, she will be afraid or anxious. If Bob believes he can become rich and important by gambling his money at a casino, it is likely that he will continue to gamble. If Bob believes it is more realistic to work and save for a better future, he will be less inclined to gamble away large sums of money. Note, it is not the gambling that causes Bob problems, but what he believes about gambling.

Thinking Comes Before Doing

I once lived in a house with a large crawl space underneath. One evening during the winter I was underneath the house using a flashlight to look for something. As I crawled farther underneath the house, I suddenly saw a snake. For me, being underneath your house on your hands and knees in the dark is not the best time to see a snake. I panicked, yelled, and started backwards as fast as I could. My heart was racing, my muscles were tense, and I was breathing hard. Most people would argue that this example breaks the ABC rule. My response appears to be automatic and beyond my control, and many would argue that this is an automatic response to seeing a snake. Some people say it is the result of millions of years of evolution while others say that God created us to respond this way toward snakes, perhaps because of the serpent in the garden, but both of these explanations are wrong. Even if the time is less than one half of a second, there is a belief that comes to mind regarding what is happening. In my case, I have a long history of not liking snakes. Many of them are poisonous and the rest are just creepy. This is what I know and believe about snakes, and in the short time between when I first saw the snake and I began to react with a panic response, my belief system kicked in. During the process of my panic, however, I began to recognize something about this particular snake—it was green. Now, if there is ever a snake I could like it would be a harmless green snake, so immediately my panic began to subside. I began to relax a little, but I still hurried out of the crawl space because even a green snake is a little creepy when it is dark and I am in a cramped space. Notice how my panic began to subside when I recognized that the snake was a harmless green snake. Furthermore, what if I had initially recognized that the snake was a toy green snake? My panic would never have occurred and I would have continued to crawl under the house. Notice carefully that as my belief about the snake changes, my response changes. Therefore, the response to A always comes through B.

In addiction, many people falsely believe certain stimuli in their environments trigger automatic responses. Addicts are constantly warned about triggers that cause them to drink alcohol, use drugs, or gamble. It is thought that if some people take one drink of alcohol, or go to a casino, or visit with certain friends, or have a bad day, that certain automatic responses take place. Many things can influence behavior, but they do not cause behavior. Things like circumstance, genetics, heredity, negative childhood experiences, and traumatic events can be very influential, but they do not produce involuntary behavior. Just because we may be inclined to respond a certain way does not mean that we are forced to give in to the inclination. This recognition ought to be the response to all genetic and brainwave arguments that are supposed to show that behavior is caused by biology. If a pedophile's brainwaves are different from normal while he views child pornography, then perhaps he should not view child pornography. If it can be proven that the genes of addicts predispose them to enjoy alcohol or certain other drugs, then perhaps they should not take those drugs or be extra cautious if they do, but it does not mean that they cannot control their behavior. The impression given by arguments and studies like this is that people are not responsible for their behavior because they may be predisposed to behave in certain ways, and this impression continues to perpetuate the myth of loss of control in addiction treatment.

Although activating events may be powerful in the way they influence people, the actual response to A always depends on what we believe about these events. So, Gilmore was mistaken in his belief that he was not thinking when he murdered two people. Over his lifetime, Gilmore developed a belief system and a seared conscience that allowed him to callously disregard the rights of others. His actions were based on what he believed about himself and his environment at the time of his actions. These beliefs were formed and validated by his actions over a long history of decision-making that ultimately led him to death row in 1977.

People often believe that cravings for drugs or alcohol are so strong that they are irresistible, but it is not the cravings themselves but what people believe about their cravings that cause them to use drugs or alcohol. Those who are chemically dependent must deal with the desire to remove the beginnings of physical withdrawal and those who are psychologically dependent must deal with negative feelings about themselves or their environments. Although these chemical and psychological cravings are different, they are not irresistible.

The Stress Connection

William Glasser (1998) makes an amazing observation regarding the power of the mind. He points out that "experiments have shown that a person who is allergic to strawberries may break out in hives when he or she goes into a room papered with strawberry-patterned wallpaper" (139). I still find it hard to believe that a biological reaction can take place just because someone sees a picture of strawberries. It is self-evident that thinking is not biology, but it seems that biology can be affected by thinking.

For years, the medical community has recognized the mind-body connection to physical health. This connection is called psychosomatic and refers to the way that our thinking can impact our health. Harold Koenig (2002) provides an interesting summary of research on the way autoimmune disorders, such as psoriasis, rheumatoid arthritis, Graves disease, and multiple sclerosis, are negatively affected by psychosocial stress (174). Stress is known to be physically harmful and there is evidence to suggest that stress management can positively impact the treatment of diseases like diabetes (186). Stress involves what takes place in our minds, or thinking, and if our minds can play such a significant role in our physical health, then surely it can significantly impact our behavior. Addiction is a behavior, and stress is a major trigger for this behavior.

If stress management is important in improving both health and behavior, then how can people manage their stress? One way is to use basic cognitive techniques that focus on our faulty thinking. A good example can be found in the book, *Stress Inoculation Training*, by Donald

Meichenbaum (1985). Another way is to recognize that stress reduction is a byproduct of biblical religion. The Bible says, "And the peace of God, which transcends all understanding, will guard your hearts and your minds in Christ Jesus" (Philippians 4:7). Our gentleness should "be evident to all" (v. 5) and we are commanded not to "be anxious" (v. 6).

When we talk about stress we are really talking about our response to difficult, irritating, or disruptive events in our lives. Stressful events are a fact of life and they cannot be avoided. There are the daily frustrations of living, like having a flat tire or major exam, and there are major life events, like getting married, changing jobs, or moving to a new location. Some life events can be even more stressful, like the death of a spouse, chronic illness, going to prison, or being in combat. Events that activate stress are not all negative. For example, getting married, having a baby, changing jobs, or moving to a new location may be very positive but still stressful. It is our perception of stressful events, however, that causes us to think, feel, and behave in certain ways that are harmful to ourselves and others.

Several years ago I remember hearing the story of a prominent educator and church leader who killed someone while driving drunk. In his explanation of how he could act in a manner so inconsistent with biblical teaching and the safety of others, he indicated that his drinking began as a way to cope with the stress of his job. It never sounded right to me; after all, he was well paid and had a secure job, so why did he need to stay drunk most of the time? Besides, there are many other people who have far greater stress than this man and yet they do not feel the need to use drugs and alcohol to cope with the stress of work. It sounded to me like just another rationalization for behaving irresponsibly. I think I would have had more respect for the man if he had just confessed, "I got drunk because I wanted to, and I am guilty of breaking the laws of God and man." Yet, this seems to be too honest and needlessly frank in today's culture. So we continue down the road of confessing on the one hand and excusing on the other.

Stress is real and can be an important addiction trigger, but it does not force anyone to consume drugs and alcohol or gamble. Drugs and alcohol can give temporary relief from stress and gambling and other addictions can provide temporary escape, but these choices have long-term negative consequences. They do nothing to solve the root cause of stress. I recommend three intervention techniques for successfully managing life's stressors. First, emphasize the B in the ABC principle and focus on your thinking. It is our perception of stressful events and not the events themselves that cause us the most difficulty. Recognize distorted beliefs and avoid catastrophic thinking; that is, do not make a mountain out of a molehill. Reframe the daily stress of living by viewing things positively; for example, when you are frustrated, think of the old saying, "A pearl is the result of an oyster's victory over an irritation." Recognize what happens to your mind, body, and feelings when you experience a stressful event. Explain to yourself what is taking place so that you can deal with it effectively without resorting to drugs, alcohol, gambling, or some other addiction. Remember, it is possible to choose the way you think about yourself, your environment, and your addiction.

Second, focus on your faith. Develop a faith perspective rather than an event perspective. Events should be viewed in the context of the greater picture, as in Paul's question, "If God is for us, who can be against us?" (Romans 8:31). So, if you are experiencing stress in your life, ask yourself the question, "What is the worst thing that can happen?" Is it death? As Christians, we should be prepared for death. If you are not prepared for the worst thing that can happen, you will always have anxiety about the future. Most of the time, however, the worst thing that can happen is only a remote possibility. In addition, our faith in God should lead us to be more positive, tolerant, forgiving, and thankful. These characteristics increase our ability to manage stress.

Finally, develop your spiritual side and get connected with your inner self. Learn to stand outside of yourself and view life from a larger, more objective perspective. If you find that your stress comes from pursuing the goals you have set for yourself, then think about reevaluating the priorities of your life, or viewing success and failure differently than you have in the past.

Learned Helplessness

Joe was a young man in his late 20s who was having life adjustment problems. He had tried several times to set a positive direction for his life but, for one reason or another, he felt he was a total failure. To combat feelings of loneliness and failure, Joe began to abuse alcohol on a regular basis. One day his drinking was especially bad and he began acting crazy and out-of-control. Someone reported Joe to the police, they arrested him, and a judge ordered a mental examination. The psychiatrist decided he needed to be on medication, so Joe was required to go to a residential treatment center where he was given medication. When I first met Joe he was sitting on a couch with his head bowed and his eyes barely opened. I tried to get him to talk but he would only say a few words. The effects of the powerful brain drugs he had been given kept him in a zombie-like state. Over the course of the next several weeks, I tried to get Joe to open up and establish eye contact with people. I also encouraged him to talk about his life in an attempt to discover what led to his current situation. In our conversations, I learned that Joe felt helpless to make changes in his life, so he was just going along with whatever people told him. I recognized that before Joe could ever function normally again, he needed to overcome his feelings of helplessness and get off the medication. His original psychotic episode was likely due to his alcohol abuse rather than schizophrenia or some other psychotic disorder. These symptoms usually disappear soon after a person stops using drugs or alcohol. Unfortunately for Joe, he was diagnosed with a psychotic disorder and was put on powerful brain drugs. It is easy to get lost in the mental health system and once a person is diagnosed and starts taking medication it can be a long time before anyone ever reexamines his condition. In Joe's case, I was the first counselor to spend more than just a few minutes with him.

Joe is a good example of someone who has experienced failure and disappointment in life and has reacted to it by giving up. He was now allowing addiction, people, and events to control his life and he appeared to be in a state of helplessness. My counseling goals were to help him overcome the negative effects of the medication so he could communicate better, change his helpless state of mind, stop his alcohol abuse, and help him discover new values and goals for his life. I became convinced that Joe's delusions and hallucinations resulted from his alcohol abuse and that the correct diagnosis according to the DSM-IV should be Substance-Induced Psychotic Disorder. This diagnosis did not warrant the powerful brain drugs he had been given, and even if he had some form of schizophrenia, these drugs may not be necessary for recovery anyway (Breggin, 1991, 1998).

Joe's problem is that he has given up on fighting for himself and he no longer believes he has the power the shape his future. Joe's helpless attitude is characteristic of many who are addicted. Sometimes this is because of repeated failed attempts to stop an addiction, or it is because of what others have told them about their own powerlessness. The belief in powerlessness is often reinforced by friends, family, medical doctors, and others who treat the addiction. Unless this belief is changed, it is unlikely they will ever change their behavior.

What if it is the case that the failure of people to recover from addiction is because of the false belief they have about themselves and their environments? What if these false beliefs arise from mistaken inferences they make about the power of drugs and their past failures to stop their addictions? When people hold pessimistic beliefs about controlling certain behaviors they enjoy, they can easily develop a helpless and hopeless view toward recovery. Instead, what if people could change pessimistic beliefs by acquiring new skills that allow them to gain personal control over addiction?

The work of Martin Seligman (1998) suggests there are two important concepts that can explain why some people become helpless and quit trying to change their behaviors. These concepts are learned helplessness and explanatory style. Learned helplessness is "the giving-up reaction, the quitting response that follows from the belief that whatever you do doesn't matter." Explanatory style is "the manner in which you habitually explain to yourself why events happen" (15). Both of these concepts are closely related, and if people want to change learned helplessness, they must change the way they explain the bad events of their lives.

Seligman discovered that if dogs were put in cages where they experienced unavoidable shock, they would soon quit trying to escape. Later, when the dogs were given the opportunity to escape, they would still endure the shock and not try to escape. It seems they had learned to remain in a state of helplessness. When the dogs had some control over escaping a shock they would not learn helplessness and continue to try and escape, but when the shock was inescapable, they would give up. Seligman applied this research to humans and found that helpless animals act like helpless humans. When people experience negative events and become convinced they have little or no control over these events, they give up trying. In humans, a key element in developing learned helplessness is explanatory style; that is, the way people explain to themselves why negative events happen. If people have a negative explanatory style they tend to get depressed and become helpless. If they have a positive explanatory style, they tend to be less depressed and more energetic in solving their problems.

The way people explain things to themselves determines how helpless or how energized they become when they encounter negative events. Seligman describes a negative explanatory style as one that is personal (It is my fault), permanent (It is always going to be like this), and pervasive (It is going to undermine every other aspect of life) (76). To illustrate, if Bill asks Ann for a date and she says no, he might personalize the rejection by thinking, "There is something wrong with me." He can make the rejection permanent by believing, "I am never going to have a girlfriend." Finally, he may allow the rejection of one woman to extend to all other women by saying, "Women hate me." In this example, Bill has the three Ps of a negative explanatory style. He has explained a negative event in terms that are personal, permanent, and pervasive.

Seligman's work in this area represents a major contribution to understanding depression. He developed a questionnaire that reveals when a person has a negative explanatory style and found that depressed people consistently explain bad events negatively, which he argues is the core of depressed thinking (58). Seligman also found that cognitive therapy could change the explanatory style of many depressed people from negative to positive, and "the more expertly it was delivered, the more thorough the change to optimism" (81). What this shows is that when people change the way they think, they can determine whether they become depressed or stay depressed.

Although Seligman's work focuses mostly on depression, his ideas can also be applied to addiction. In fact, I would argue that depression is like addiction in that it begins with the way we think about problems of living. If we are pessimists, we tend to give up and become depressed. Those who are pessimistic and depressed are more likely to engage in addictions because they are unhappy with the way they view themselves. Addiction is a way for people to distract themselves from their strong negative feelings by providing either an escape or a temporary way to feel differently. Soon, they begin to falsely believe they are unable to deal with unpleasant events and negative feelings unless they engage in their addictions.

There are some interesting parallels between addiction and

depression. The cognitive approach to depression suggests that if we change our thinking we can change the way we feel, whereas the medical community often views depression as a chemical or biological problem that is to be treated with drugs. Likewise, addiction is often viewed as a disease, or a biological response that is automatic and beyond one's control rather than a cognitive choice that one makes.

Unlearning Helplessness

Research has shown that optimism is beneficial to good physical and mental health. For example, the immune system of optimistic people seems to work better than pessimists, which means they tend to catch fewer infectious diseases. Optimistic people also tend to live longer than pessimists. People who are optimistic are less likely to use addiction as an escape from unpleasantness because they are more active and energetic about solving their problems. Optimistic people are less likely to use drugs and alcohol to make them feel better because they are less depressed and already feel better than those who are pessimistic. With all of these advantages, common sense should demand that addiction treatment should begin from an optimistic perspective, but it is hard to imagine a more pessimistic view of behavior than the disease model of addiction. First, addicts are expected to explain their addiction in negative terms, which follows the negative explanatory style model. Addiction is personalized in that addicts are told they have a physical, biological, or genetic defect that causes their behavior. It is permanent in that addicts must recognize they have a permanent allergy to alcohol, drugs, gambling, or any other behavior labeled as a disease by the proponents of the disease model. Regardless of how many years they do not engage in the behaviors, they are still required to say negative and self-defeating statements about themselves because of their past behaviors. It is pervasive in that the disease label affects every other aspect of their lives. Any other behavior the addict enjoys now becomes a potential addiction. The negative explanatory style is reinforced by AA and the Twelve Steps theory when addicts are encouraged to believe in helplessness as a part of their recovery, which encourages them to become even more passive in the treatment process.

Seligman argues that helplessness can be cured if people become convinced their own actions now work (67), which means they must be convinced they can still do things that can make a difference. To illustrate,

George came to me for help with a nicotine addiction. His efforts in the past ended in failure and he is now convinced that he cannot stop smoking. My approach to George was to teach him how to overcome his learned helplessness by giving him a task that he could accomplish. Instead of quitting nicotine, I suggested he practice harm reduction. Instead of twelve cigarettes a day, I suggested that he smoke ten. He agreed to try this and he was successful in smoking two cigarettes less per day. His confidence was restored by this success and he was able to make further reductions over time. For George, I never recommended total abstinence because the goal was to reduce the harm and unlearn his helplessness. Had the goal been total abstinence, it is likely that he would have failed again as he had done many times in the past. After George unlearns his helplessness, he can then examine his past failures for clues as to their cause and learn how to view his failures in a non-negative way. Knowledge is empowering, and if people understand why they fail they can make adjustments the next time they try. If they can unlearn their helplessness, they will continue to try in the future.

Learned optimism is the opposite of learned helplessness. Seligman points out that learned optimism is not the power of positive thinking, where people try to believe upbeat statements about themselves in the absence of evidence, but learning not to think negatively by adopting a positive explanatory style (221). For example, to what do you attribute the negative events of your life? Do you blame yourself for everything bad that happens? Do you allow one negative event to expand to other areas of your life? So, if Bill is turned down by Ann when he asks her out, he should look for an explanation that does not personalize the event, which means that he should not blame himself. Perhaps Ann is married or already has a boyfriend, or perhaps she has other plans. These alternative explanations allow Bill to believe that his actions still matter, which encourages him to ask other women for dates in the future.

An example of optimism in the Bible is Paul's statement, "I can do all things through him who gives me strength" (Philippians 4:13). Learned helplessness would say, "I can do nothing through him who gives me strength."

Conclusion

The essence of the ABCs of addiction is that people's beliefs are connected to their addictions. There are no automatic and predetermined responses. As long as people falsely believe they have involuntary responses to life situations they will continue to have behavior problems. Gary Gilmore's mistaken belief that he was not thinking but doing is common among those who have alcohol, drug, gambling, sex, and other addictions. Gilmore's belief that rage is not reason assumes that emotions are not a response to beliefs. Instead, it is what we believe about the events that happen to us, and not the events themselves, that cause us to respond the way we do. Likewise, drugs, alcohol, and gambling do not cause people to become addicted; instead, it is what people believe about these behaviors that determines whether they continue the behaviors. People may be completely unaware of their set of beliefs, or they may not understand the relationship between their beliefs and their addictions, but these beliefs are the essential component of their addiction and this should be the target of focus in treatment and recovery.

Learned helplessness is a false belief that perpetuates addiction and, unfortunately, is a belief that is often reinforced in addiction treatment. When people accept the negative statements said by themselves and others regarding their addiction, or when they experience failure in stopping an addiction, they may develop learned helplessness.

Recommended Reading

One of the best explanations of the ABC model of cognitive therapy is by Rian McMullin (2000) in his book, *The New Handbook of Cognitive Therapy Techniques*. Although this book was originally designed for therapists, the material is presented on a level that makes the subject understandable by those who have no training in counseling. In addition to the ABC model, McMullin discusses many other important cognitive techniques that benefit all those who are searching for more effective ways to help themselves and others. Although the concept of learned helplessness as developed by Martin Seligman (*Learned Optimism: How to Change Your Mind and Your Life*, 1998) did not originally focus on addiction treatment, a relevant application can be made in this area. I would also recommend reading his other two books, *Authentic Happiness* (2002) and *What You Can Change...And What You Can't* (1998). Addiction recovery can be positively affected by concepts found in all three of these books.

Questions for Discussion

1.   Why is anger not an example of an automatic response?

2. Give some examples of unconventional values that others may have that you do not. How does this knowledge contribute to an understanding of addiction?

3. Discuss an event in your life that was very important to you at the time but now you view the event much differently. What does this tell you about the impact your beliefs have on the way you respond to life events?

4. Discuss and apply the ABC model to events in your own life. How would knowing about this model have helped you with some issues in your past?

5. Explain how one's belief about alcohol is more important than the drug itself. How can beliefs affect those who are physically addicted to alcohol? What is the difference between a physical and a psychological addiction to alcohol? How can our beliefs affect both?

6. What is learned helplessness and how can we learn it and unlearn it? How is the concept of learned helplessness related to addiction?

7. What is the connection of stress to addiction and other behaviors?

Chapter 6
Gambling and Addiction

Welcome to Las Vegas

When most people think about gambling they think of Las Vegas. My first visit to Las Vegas occurred in the mid 1990s while on vacation. We were supposed to meet up with other family members at a casino and then drive to California for a family reunion. Our plans were to eat at a buffet inside a casino and then be on our way. Our biggest mistake was trying to do this on the weekend when the casinos were at their maximum occupancy. The traffic was congested, the building was packed, and the buffet line was too long. We decided to head out of town and pick up something to eat on the way. Personally, I was glad to be heading out of town, and as we were heading out of the city I said to myself, "I had just as soon never come this way again." Like many people, I could not imagine living in a place that had the nickname of "Sin City," but through time and circumstance, I found myself moving to Las Vegas in July, 1999.

The reputation of this city far exceeds the reality, and I found Las Vegas to be no more evil than other great cities in the United States. Except for gambling and tourism, Las Vegas is like any other large city in the southwestern United States. The thing that distinguishes Las Vegas from most other cities is that gambling is just about everywhere, including places like grocery stores and restaurants. Casinos along the strip are mostly for tourists, but local casinos are found all around the city. Casinos in Las Vegas are major centers of entertainment and even if you do not gamble you will find yourself going to a casino to visit a restaurant, movie theater, bowling alley, ice skating rink, concert, art museum, or shopping mall.

I understand that about 20% of the adults who live here have a problem with gambling. I have never seen any scientific research to back up this estimate, but in my own experience I have observed that gambling addiction is greater here than in other parts of the country. This may be due to the availability of gambling as an addiction outlet; for example, people in other parts of the country may have other outlets for addictive behavior. It could also be the case that people who are prone to addiction and gambling may be drawn to the city. For example, nicotine and alcohol flow freely in all casinos in Las Vegas and a high percentage of people who gamble also smoke and drink. People who tend to give themselves over to all kinds of addictions, like drugs, alcohol, nicotine, pornography, and so forth, also like to gamble.

Gambling addiction is also a greater problem in the church in Las Vegas than in other parts of the country. It is not because people are tempted by the casinos beyond that which they can bear, but because the opportunity to engage in a gambling addiction is greater here than in other places. Perhaps Christians in Tennessee and Texas have problems with other kinds of addictions. To illustrate, a young man in Las Vegas may suffer negative consequences because he spends too much money gambling while a young man in Arkansas may suffer negative consequences because he spends too much on hunting and fishing.

Is Gambling a Sin?

After moving to Las Vegas, I had to decide how I would handle the gambling issue. Should I preach against gambling? Several members of the church where I preach work in some capacity for the gaming industry, so should I also preach against working at casinos? Most of the Christians I work with never gamble, but occasionally, I will hear about some church members who enjoy playing the slot machines, and I am aware of a few who enjoy playing blackjack and poker. So, is gambling a sin like adultery or drunkenness?

Gambling is a behavior, and before a behavior can be labeled as a sin, it is important to define the behavior one has in mind. For this book I will follow the definition given by Ladouceur and Doucet (1998), which is similar to most of the other definitions by people who study this behavior. Gambling consists of three criteria: 1) players gamble money or an object of value; 2) the bet is irreversible once it is placed; and 3) the outcome of the wager relies on chance (5). Some games, like poker and blackjack, require skill in addition to chance. Some slot machine games, like video poker, give the illusion of a required skill by giving the player a chance to provide input.

Since I profess to be a Bible preacher, I strongly believe it is important to give a Bible answer to every issue, just as the Bible says, "Always be prepared to give an answer to everyone who asks you to give the reason for the hope that you have" (1 Peter 3:15). The subject of gambling, however, is not addressed in the Bible and games that involve the above three criteria are nowhere labeled as sin. So, I will be happy to preach against gambling when I find it condemned in Scripture.

Realizing that many preachers like to preach against this behavior, I decided to do an internet search of some popular sermon websites to see if perhaps I have missed something in my search of the Scriptures. What I found was that many preachers would begin their sermon by admitting that the Bible says nothing about this subject and then proceed to present an entire lesson based on opinion rather than biblical teaching. One preacher suggested that although the Bible does not address this subject, we are supposed to discern the teaching by looking at passages that have nothing to do with the behavior, which seems to me to be a dangerous way to apply Scripture. However, out of deference to these preachers, and out of concern for those who listen to them, I will discuss some of the arguments made by those who preach against gambling.

1. Gambling is stealing by consent. I am not really sure about the point being made here since, by definition, stealing is without consent. Taking something of value from someone with their consent is receiving a gift. Winning a prize is where people engage in a behavior with mutual consent where the outcome is based on chance. The stealing argument seems to refer to the supposed wrongness of someone willingly placing a wager. Preachers who make this point usually give an analogy to other sins that we willfully do, such as adultery, but adultery is clearly prohibited in Scripture while gambling is not. The analogy, therefore, is comparing apples to oranges. Yes, adultery is by consent, and if it were not, the behavior could not be defined as adultery.

2. Gambling is contrary to good stewardship. It is true that we are to be good stewards of material things (Luke 16:11), but this applies to how we use our financial resources in general and not to any specific behavior. I could argue that buying a diamond ring is a waste of financial resources, but most people believe they have the right to set aside money for such a purpose, especially if they want to get married, or to please a spouse on an anniversary occasion. I also believe that buying a bass boat is a poor use of financial resources, but there are many Christians in Arkansas, Texas, Tennessee, and elsewhere who believe they have the right to take a portion of their income and waste it on such a thing. I would never make a purchase like this because I do not enjoy the hobby, but it is going too far for me to label this behavior as sin just because I do not enjoy it. I do not enjoy playing slot machines or poker, but some people do, and they set aside a certain amount to spend on this hobby every year. It is a matter of judgment as to how much money spent on such a hobby becomes a poor use of one's financial resources. It is likely that a vacation trip to Hawaii costs more than a gambling trip to Las Vegas, but it is binding where God has not bound to say that one is a sin and the other is not.

3. Gambling contradicts the work ethic. Work is honorable and good for all Christians (Ephesians 4:28). Work is not a curse because of sin but a blessing from God. Before Adam and Eve sinned, they were told to work in the garden (Genesis 2:15). Not working is contrary to God's plan, and Paul gave this rule to the church: "If a man will not work, he shall not eat" (2 Thessalonians 3:10). It is the opinion of some preachers, however, that gamblers are lazy and do not want to work for a living, but this is assigning a motive to those who gamble that most do not have. Perhaps the preacher knows more gamblers than I do, but the people I know who enjoy gambling are not lazy. The people I know who gamble do so because they enjoy playing games of chance and they do not mind wagering money on those games.

4. Gamblers are greedy. This may be true with some gamblers, but it is also true with people who never gamble. Some people work two jobs because they are greedy, but work is honorable. Some people save their money and invest because they are greedy, but saving and investing are not sins. The Bible says "the love of money is a root of all kinds of evil" (1 Timothy 6:10), and some who gamble do commit evil because of their love for money, but it is wrong to assign evil motives to everyone because of what some do.

5. Gambling violates the Golden Rule. Jesus said, "So in everything, do to others what you would have them do to you, for this sums up the Law and the Prophets" (Matthew 7:12). The idea of doing unto others what you would have them do to you is called the Golden Rule. Since gamblers seek to win money from the casinos, they are supposedly violating this rule. I am sure that casino executives here in Las Vegas are delighted to know that some preachers are taking an interest in their welfare, but in reply, they would say not to worry because they are doing just fine. Some of the most beautiful buildings in the world are owned by casinos in Las Vegas, and some of the casino buildings cost over a billion dollars! They did not build these palaces because you win but because you lose. The odds are always in favor of the casinos.

6. *Gambling demonstrates a lack of self-control.* Paul said, "I will not be mastered by anything" (1 Corinthians 6:12). Certainly, this can include gambling behavior, but it can also include other behaviors, like eating, shopping, working, playing, sleeping, and so forth. People who are addicted to gambling are out of control, but people who are addicted to eating and shopping are also out of control. Gambling and casinos do not cause addiction—people cause addiction. Losing control is a choice one can make, but it does not necessarily mean that the behavior itself is wrong.

Gambling Addiction

How do you define a problem gambler? The American Psychiatric Association (2000) provides a diagnostic criteria for what they call pathological gambling in their book, *Diagnostic and Statistical Manual of Mental Disorders* (674). The 2000 edition of this book is commonly referred to as the DSM IV. Pathological comes from the Greek word *pathos* and refers to strong desires or feelings. The three occurrences of this word in the Greek New Testament have a sexual context and are translated in the NIV as either lust or passion (Romans 1:26; Colossians 3:5; 1 Thessalonians 4:5). The use of *pathos* in pathological refers to the passion for gambling that is so strong for some people that they choose to gamble even though it causes them problems. Some would argue that the desire to gamble is so strong that they cannot control their behavior, but this is one of the myths brought over from the disease model of addiction. The reality is, there is no involuntary human response to being exposed to a game. Games are fun and exciting and people enjoy playing them, but there is no game that forces people to do things.

Pathological gambling is listed under the heading of Impulse Control Disorders in the DSM IV. This fits nicely with the definition of an addiction as discussed in chapter 1, which is a compulsion to do something despite the negative consequences. For a variety of reasons, and over the course of a long decision-making process, many people arrive at a point in their lives where they choose not to exercise control over their behaviors despite the damage it brings to their personal lives. Unfortunately, the use of some terminology in the addiction field gives the impression that people cannot control their behaviors. For example, consider the definition of pathological gambling by Reber and Reber (2001): "An impulse control disorder characterized by chronic inability to resist impulses to gamble" (292). People may behave in such a way that it appears to some observers that they do not have the ability to control their behaviors but this is not what is taking place. Instead, some people choose not to exercise control over their gambling behavior because they believe they will find greater pleasure in the immediate gratification of gambling than in the benefits of not gambling. Thankfully, the DSM IV does not list "inability to resist impulses" as a criterion of pathological gambling, and the use of this terminology comes from the disease model and the Twelve Steps theory of alcohol abuse. Many psychological and environmental factors can enter in the kinds of decisions people make about gambling, including self-deception, but people ultimately make their own choices about what they value and how they behave.

People are labeled as pathological gamblers if they have five or more of the following DSM IV diagnostic criteria:

1. *Preoccupation*: The individual is preoccupied with gambling by reliving past gambling experiences or planning a future gambling experience.

2. *Tolerance*: There is a need to gamble more often and with greater amounts of money to achieve the desired amount of satisfaction.

3. *Unsuccessful efforts to stop*: In disease model literature, this criterion is usually listed as "loss of control." However, all the DSM IV states for the third criterion is "has repeated unsuccessful efforts to control, cut back, or stop gambling" (674). There is a big difference in an individual being unable to control a behavior and having failed to control a behavior. Failing to control behavior implies choice, but being unable to control behavior implies that people have no choice. The belief in loss of control is a self-defeating belief that hinders change. Instead, the treatment strategy ought to be to help people discover why they have failed in their

past efforts to stop gambling rather than the belief that they cannot control their behaviors.

4. *Withdrawal*: Some people become restless and irritable when they try to stop gambling. There is nothing unusual in this. It is common for people to become restless, irritable, and upset when they experience strong emotions. Likewise, when people have a passion for gambling, they experience some discomfort when they deprive themselves of this behavior, but they will not die or go berserk if they do not gamble.

5. *Escape*: When people are experiencing strong negative feelings, or when they are unhappy with something in their environment, they may gamble as a way to escape unpleasantness.

6. *Chasing losses*: Chasing losses is the practice of gambling more money after a major loss in an effort to win back the amount of the loss.

7. *Lying about gambling*: Some people lie to family members and others about their losses and involvement in gambling.

8. *Illegal acts*: Because of heavy losses, some people commit illegal acts like forgery, fraud, theft, and embezzlement to finance gambling activities.

9. *Jeopardize relationships*: This occurs when people lose significant family and work relationships because of gambling. They may also forfeit important educational and career opportunities because of gambling.

10. *Borrows from others*: When people get in a desperate financial condition because of gambling losses, they may turn to friends and relatives to borrow money.

The Games People Play

When I lived in Texas I would occasionally buy a lottery ticket. Thankfully, here in Nevada we do not have a state lottery so I am never tempted to do this anymore. People used to wonder why I would buy only one ticket since I could greatly increase my chances by buying a large number of tickets. I recognized, however, that the chances of me ever winning the lottery were so slim that even if I bought a thousand tickets it would require divine intervention for me to have any reasonable chance of winning. So, if God wants me to win, how many tickets do you think I am going to have to buy? This is why I have never been able to understand why people of faith would ever have a problem with gambling. For believers, pathological gambling is really a faith problem and not a gambling problem. You should not have to throw away your life's savings on the lottery or in a casino before you realize that God is not going to intervene on your behalf!

At the time, however, I felt it was worth the measly price of a lottery ticket so that I could have the pleasure of dreaming about what I would do with all of that money. I used to do the same thing when I would gamble the price of a postage stamp for my chance to enter the Publisher's Clearinghouse Sweepstakes. It allowed me the pleasure of dreaming a little and this is why many enjoy some forms of gambling. I remember once seeing a news story about a woman who had become very successful in her business. The reporter asked her about how her new found wealth had changed her life, and she said, "Well, I never send in those sweepstakes entries anymore!" Wealthy people who are satisfied with their financial success never gamble because of some financial dream, but dreams are not the only reason people gamble; for example, some people enjoy taking risks while others just like to play games.

Although the state of Nevada does not have a lottery, we do have what is called the Mega Bucks Jackpot. This is where all the casinos link together with certain slot machines in each casino and offer a huge jackpot for the lucky winner. One day after I finished eating at a casino buffet, I noticed the Mega Bucks Jackpot was close to $20 million. Now, I never waste my time playing if the jackpot is only $7 or $8 million, but $20 million really gets my attention! Following my belief in the necessity of divine intervention, I said to my wife, "I think I will play once." So, I put in the required $3 and hit the button and...I won! No, I did not win the Mega Bucks Jackpot, but only a lesser prize of $50. The Mega Bucks slots are enticing because they will let you win small amounts on your way to the big jackpot. Well, I am not really interested in small amounts because I am after the big money, so I decided to play again, especially since I could play from my winnings and not from my own money. After two more unsuccessful plays, I won again...not the jackpot but another $50. I thought to myself, "Man, I am on a roll, I have nearly a $100 in winnings so far!" So, I decided to play again in pursuit of the big jackpot, but then I began to think, "I have just violated my own rule about gambling and I have been deceived by the excitement of a couple of small wins." For me to win the Mega Bucks Jackpot will require divine intervention and I do not believe God needs me to increase the odds by continuing to play. So, I took my small winnings and went home.

One of the worst things that can happen to you in a casino is to win, and the more you win the more you are attracted to gambling. The thrill of winning several hundred or several thousand dollars is very exciting and it gives many people a rush more powerful than drugs. The casino executives know this, so they program their slot machines to let you win. Many slots have a 90% payout; that is, on average, for every $100 you play you will win $90, but constantly exchanging $100 for $90 will make the casino rich and you poor. So, how are most people able to gamble without having problems? They decide how much money they are going to throw away at a slot machine before they ever enter the casino, and when that is gone, they walk away.

Sitting for hours in front of a slot machine and gambling several thousand dollars is not appealing to me, but it really provides pleasure for some people. This is brought to my attention every Tuesday in Las Vegas as I go down to one of the local casinos for our weekly church breakfast. To get to the buffet, you have to walk through the gaming area, and every week, at about 7:30 AM in the morning, there are hundreds of people sitting around the casino playing the slot machines. Why are these people there at this time of the day? I can understand gambling at night, or on the weekend, but who would want to gamble early in the morning on a weekday? I often want to survey the gamblers and see just what it is that causes them to be there at that time of the day. Because the casino where we have breakfast is off the strip, many of the people are probably local residents who just enjoy gambling at that time of the day. Others may be from out of town but they prefer to be away from the hustle and bustle of the strip. Perhaps they have saved all year just to spend a few days gambling in Las Vegas.

Casinos in Las Vegas do not have locks on their doors and they stay open twenty-four hours a day, seven days a week, which suggests that there are many people who enjoy gambling at all times of the day or night. Just because I cannot appreciate the pleasure this brings some people does not mean that I have the right to judge them for what they enjoy doing. From a biblical standpoint, I am not willing to argue that wasting $3,000 on a gambling trip to Las Vegas is evil while wasting $3,000 on a hunting trip to Colorado is good. If wasting money is a sin then all Christians need to stop taking vacations and going out to eat. Devoting a portion of your budget to recreation is not a sin, and the key to almost any activity is common sense, moderation, and self-control.

Why is it that some people allow themselves to be destroyed because of gambling? This result is not unique to gambling, and the same question can be asked about a number of other self-destructive behaviors. With regards to gambling, however, a key mental distortion is the failure to take in account the reality of the odds against winning (Ladouceur, Sylvain, and Doucet, 1998). To illustrate, Ciarrocchi (2002) gives a helpful example of odds that should give most people a reality check on the chances of winning big. For example, the odds of being murdered in the next year are 1 in 11,000. I did not know the odds of being murdered were that high, and I am sure the odds are greater in certain parts of the country than in others, but even at 1 in 11,000 it is very unlikely that you will be murdered in the coming year. Some of you who are reading this may have known a friend or relative who was murdered, but I have never known or even met someone who was later murdered. People die every year after they have been struck by lightning, but the odds of you dying this year from a lightning strike are only 1 in 750,000. Imagine 750,000 people, which is the size of a major city in the United States, and the odds of being the one who is struck by lightning. The odds are so small that most would not even worry about it. In contrast, the odds of winning the Powerball Jackpot are 1 in 80,000,000!

Mental Trash

A cognitive distortion occurs when we believe something that is not true. It is the mental trash that clutters up our mind with false ideas about reality and keeps us from feeling, thinking, and behaving as we should. A cognitive distortion can be completely false, or it can contain an element of truth, but the truth is exaggerated or interpreted in such a way that it becomes false.

Once, when I was in college, I was riding along in my car when suddenly a large cloud of smoke started to come out from under the hood. I told my friend, "Well, this is it, the motor is ruined and I might as well call a junkyard to come and get it." My friend suggested that he look at the motor first, so he opened the hood and examined the motor. He discovered that a small hose that connects the water pump to the manifold had burst. The escaping radiator fluid was spraying on the hot motor and causing all of the smoke. We walked to a nearby auto parts store and purchased the hose connection for a few dollars and fixed the problem. My response to this situation is a classic example of what cognitive psychologists call catastrophic thinking; that is, I imagined the situation to be far worse than it actually was. Catastrophic thinking causes people pain and anxiety, but it is only one of the many cognitive distortions that negatively impact people's lives.

Cognitive or thinking distortions are at the heart of gambling addiction, which helps explain why gambling addicts continue in behaviors that often defy common sense. It is like a boxer who is knocked down again and again but keeps coming back for more. Most people recognize the futility of destructive behavior long before the addict does, which is why most people are not gambling addicts. So, why is it the case that the gambling addict cannot see what others can see despite being repeatedly punished by losing greater and greater amounts of money? The key difference between pathological gamblers and those who control the amount they gamble is what is believed about gambling behavior. Those who continue to lose money in violation of the obvious laws of learning and rationality continue to do so because they have deceived themselves about what they are doing. A survey of problem gamblers by Toneatto and colleagues (1997) revealed a number of different categories of cognitive distortions related to gambling. To get the participants to reveal their beliefs, researchers asked the question, "Do you do anything specifically to increase your chance of winning?" (256). In games of chance that do not require skill, this is a ridiculous question to ask since there is nothing that can be done to improve the chances of winning, but gambling addicts always believe they have some control over chance. Let us now examine some of the mental trash that contributes to the problem gambler's deception.

1. Cues: Cues consists of wagers based on subjective feelings called hunches, omens, or instinct. For a person to have a beneficial hunch regarding a game of chance would require an act of God. All other hunches, omens, and feelings are nonsense.

2. Testing: Hypothesis testing is based on the belief that a person has special knowledge of ways to win but he must first go and test it. The problem is that during the testing process, he forgets about the test and continues to gamble despite mounting losses. For example, some religious gamblers pray to God for success but then keep on gambling when God does not answer their prayers with a win. Others test their hypothesis, but when it fails, they make up another test.

3. *Mind control*: This is the false belief that people can improve their odds by thinking positively about outcomes. A positive mental attitude is worthless and never increases odds in a game of chance.

4. *Behaviors and rituals*: This is the belief that certain behaviors and rituals can influence outcomes of chance. For example, gambling at a certain place or time, wearing certain clothes, or repeating lucky phrases. The practice of picking the number for a lottery ticket is an example and is based on the false belief that the gambler's personal choice can influence chance. For this reason, I never tried to pick the numbers of a lottery ticket because I knew that my numbers were no better than other numbers, and to believe so is to believe a lie.

5. *Luck as a state*: Luck is viewed as a state of being, as in, "I am lucky today" or "I am lucky on weekends." Some falsely view themselves as being able to improve their luck, or make themselves luckier than others. There is no such thing as being in a state of good luck or being lucky.

6. *Probability errors*: Problem gamblers tend to misunderstand the laws of probability. If a gambler has just lost $1,000 at a slot machine, he may falsely believe that the odds are now in his favor at this machine. The false belief that winning is imminent after large losses is called chasing losses. The illusion of possible control over the laws of probability and chance is a fundamental flaw, but that which ought to be evident to everyone is not to the problem gambler. To illustrate, in one study of gamblers in England, problem gamblers believed that winning at slot machines was mostly the result of skill rather than chance and this belief was the difference between pathological and nonpathological gamblers (Ciarrocchi, 2002).

7. *Memory biases*: When people enjoy doing something, they tend not to think about how much it is costing. In gambling, people remember their winnings and try to forget their losses.

Deception is a characteristic of humankind and both Isaiah and Jesus warned of the possibility that "You will be ever hearing but never understanding; you will be ever seeing but never perceiving" (Matthew 13:14). Anyone can become deceived about almost anything and so there is a need for constant vigilance as people live their lives. It is not gambling, but the mental trash of distortion, denial, exaggeration, and superstition that cause people to keep hurting themselves and others.

How to Stop Gambling

Gambling is a behavior, and all behaviors can be controlled. Gambling behavior is not as irresistible and powerful as some people think, and the following suggestions may be helpful in changing a problem behavior.

1. Prepare your mind. It is not gambling, but what people believe about gambling that causes them problems, which is why introspection and self-examination are generally lacking among problem gamblers. The Bible says, "Examine yourselves to see whether you are in the faith; test yourselves" (2 Corinthians 13:5). Self-examination and introspection are essential in getting rid of the mental trash that causes harmful behavior.

The myth of loss of control is the first mental trash that needs to be thrown out. The reality is that people choose to behave this way, and for them to stop they must first prepare their minds for action. Past failures to stop gambling should not be interpreted as the inability to stop. A failure means that what you tried did not work and not that you cannot stop. When negative and self-defeating beliefs are formed about behavior they ensure that no changes will ever take place. So, clear your mind of mental trash and start thinking differently.

2. Change from a worldly focus to a spiritual focus. Problem gamblers have a worldly focus; that is, they only see the immediate gratification of the moment. Drugs enhance the worldly focus, and there is a strong correlation between alcohol consumption and gambling, so get off all drugs, including alcohol, caffeine, and nicotine. This would also include prescription stimulants, depressants, and mood altering drugs. This action clears your mind so that you can have a more objective view of your behavior. The Bible says, "prepare your minds for action; be self-controlled; set your hope fully on the grace to be given you when Jesus Christ is revealed" (1 Peter 1:13). Notice that discipline follows the preparation of the mind. Notice also that we are to set our hope on something that is outside of ourselves. For Christians, this means putting your life in the context of the return of Christ. Biblical spirituality is the ability to put your life in the broader context of the biblical teaching

101

about Christ, which means that you must move beyond the worldly focus of your present life so you can view things from God's perspective. This also means that our primary focus should be spiritual rather than worldly (see chapter 2), and this new perspective enables us to make the necessary changes in our behavior.

3. Avoid negative beliefs. Forget the Twelve Steps theory, GA, and the disease model of addiction and just deal with your gambling issues. Your genes, brainwaves, and illnesses do not make you gamble. When it comes to your behavior, you are neither sick nor helpless. If you believe you are both, then it is unlikely you will ever control your gambling.

4. Exercise your willpower. In his book on problem gamblers, Ciarrocchi argues that "self-regulation works like a muscle" (57). This is true, and every time you exercise self-control your willpower is strengthened. Every time you give in to temptation, or run willy nilly down the street to the first casino you can find, your willpower gets weaker. Your willpower is not weak because you are sick, but because you do not exercise it. Mariana Valverde (1998) calls the failure to exercise one's willpower a disease of the will, and "the will's capacity for freedom can only be built up by freely exercising that very will, however diseased or out of shape it might be" (33). To me, this sounds a lot like biblical teaching. Paul said the grace of God "teaches us to say 'No' to ungodliness and worldly passions, and to live self-controlled, upright and godly lives in this present age" (Titus 2:12). Those who do not practice self-control will not say "No" to their passions and impulses will always have a weak will.

Instead of saying, "I cannot control my gambling and therefore cannot go near a casino," I would argue that it would be far better to strengthen your weak will by exercising your choice. First, make up your mind about what your behavior will be before you visit a casino. If you are still unsure, take a friend with you. Walk all around the casino and observe the gambling that is taking place, and then walk out. After you do this a few times, your confidence will be strengthened about your ability to resist gambling. Next, take $20 in the casino and gamble it away. You have to decide beforehand, however, that when the $20 is gone, you will walk away. You also need to decide when to walk away if you happen to win some money. For example, if you win $50 before you gamble away the $20, then you must quit. Discipline needs to be created on the winning side as well as the losing side. As the song says, you have to "know when to hold them, and know when to fold them." This is a discipline that most recreational gamblers practice and it is one that distinguishes them from problem gamblers. It is also a discipline that strengthens the will and it will impact every other aspect of life.

5. *Do not be afraid.* Stop running and hiding every time you see a slot machine or a casino. Do not live in fear of a possible environmental stimulus that might trigger your desire to gamble. Gamblers cannot avoid all temptation to gamble so deal with it by learning to cope with and control your impulses. The Bible says, "God did not give us a spirit of timidity, but a spirit of power, of love and of self-discipline" (2 Timothy 1:7). So, do not live the rest of your life in fear of your own behavior. Do not admit to yourself and others that you are powerless or helpless to control your behavior. Do not admit to being sick and then become passive in your treatment as if you are not in control of your own destiny. Instead, face your fears, weaknesses, and problem behaviors and learn to think, feel, and behave differently.

Rian McMullin (2000, 2005) tells the story of lion behavior on the Serengeti plains of Africa. Old lions would roar on one side of a ravine to frighten the antelope to the other side where the young lions were waiting. If the antelope had run to the roar, instead of away from it, they could have escaped. People with behavioral and emotional issues are often afraid to face their problems directly and they try to run away. The problem is that the more they run away, the more afraid and weak they become. If you face your gambling problems by confronting them, you can learn to deal with them more effectively than if you live in fear. For example, you may have to prove to yourself that casinos, slot machines, and gambling friends cannot force you to do anything. One way to do this is by a gradual exposure that allows you to make a perceptual shift in your belief over time.

Conclusion

Playing games of chance for money is a behavior that many people find enjoyable. Some people, however, choose not to control their gambling and they often fail in their attempts to stop or cut back. Although disease model proponents argue that some people cannot control their gambling behavior, the DSM IV does not mention "loss of control" or "inability to stop" as a diagnostic criterion of pathological gambling. Past failures at stopping a behavior do not mean that people are unable to stop. It is not gambling, but what we believe about gambling, that causes us to give in to the impulse to gamble, and beliefs are what distinguishes problem gamblers from those who control their behavior. For example, an important false belief that normally distinguishes problem gamblers from others is the belief that they can influence the laws of probability.

Although some people gamble because of greed and the desire to get something for nothing, others do not. For some people, gambling is a way to escape some unpleasant situation. Many people gamble because of the rush they get when they win and the excitement of risking their money, while others just enjoy playing games. So, the motivation to wager a sum of money in a game of chance is complex.

Recommended Reading

Very little has been written on the subject of problem gambling. One of the better overall books on the subject is *Counseling Problem Gamblers* by Joseph Ciarrocchi (2002). Since problem gamblers have trouble with false beliefs and mental processing, any good book on cognitive psychology would be beneficial. Biblical teaching on worldliness and spirituality would benefit problem gamblers by helping them to keep life in perspective. Note, for example, the parables of the rich fool (Luke 12:13-21) and the lost son (Luke 15:11-30). Paul's discussion of the fruit of the Spirit (Galatians 5:16-26) is also helpful in understanding the difference between a worldly and a spiritual focus.

Questions for Discussion

1. How do you define gambling?
2. Discuss the different games of chance. Which ones require skill and which ones do not?
3. What does the Bible say about gambling? Is it a sin to gamble?
4. What is the key belief that distinguishes problem gamblers from people who control their gambling?
5. Discuss some of the cognitive distortions that problem gamblers have about gambling. How could educated people believe such things?
6. Is luck a state (as in "She is a lucky woman" or "I am lucky today")? If not, then explain why this is not the case.
7. Discuss the difference between a worldly focus and a spiritual focus. Why do problem gamblers have a worldly focus?

8. Why is there a correlation between consuming alcohol and gambling? The percentage of smokers is also higher among problem gamblers than those who are not. Why would this be the case?

9. Are there some common threads of belief found in all addictive behaviors? If so, what are they?

Chapter 7
Contemplating Change

Behavior Determines Identity

If an individual has an addiction identity, he tends to behave in the ways in keeping with his identity. He may continue to suffer the negative consequences of his addiction by alternating between periods of abstinence and periods of relapse. As long as he stubbornly refuses to change the false perceptions he has about himself, he continues to damage his health, relationships, and job. When a person develops an addiction identity he sometimes holds on to this identity despite all of the problems it causes. The best solution, therefore, is for people to realize the need for a strong new identity that enables them to change from addiction to self-control.

Names become important when we think about identity. The people in the Bible seemed to be more aware of the significance of identity than we are today. Parents named their children with names that had special meanings. Sometimes, people would be assigned names based on their behaviors or expected behaviors. For example, the Hebrew name translated Joshua in our English Bibles means salvation. The name also appears in the Greek New Testament and is translated Jesus in our English Bibles. Names in the Bible were important because they often conveyed something significant about the person who had the name. When the angel of the Lord informed Joseph regarding the pregnancy of Mary, the angel said, "She will give birth to a son, and you are to give him the name Jesus, because he will save his people from their sins" (Matthew 1:21). Later, Matthew tells us that people will call Jesus Immanuel, which means "God with us" (v. 23). Another example is the name of Abraham. God changed his name from Abram to Abraham because Abraham meant "father of many nations" (Genesis 17:4-5). This name change reflected the promise of God to Abraham that he would have many descendents. The name also gave him an identity that would remind him of this promise. All of these examples suggest that names can say something about expected or current behavior.

Today, we do not seem to be as concerned about names as the people were in the Bible, but we do like to label people, and by labeling people we reinforce negative stereotypes of personal behavior. This was brought to my attention when I visited a group therapy session for those who were supposed to be recovering addicts. Again and again I heard people repeat negative statements about themselves as if this is supposed to help them stay free from drugs. They would say, "My name is _____ and I am a drug addict/alcoholic." Conversations in the group also focused on other negative aspects of their past lives, which all leads to a continuous reinforcement of an addiction identity among those who participate. If people are told again and again that they are defective, diseased, and cannot control their behaviors, then we should not be surprised when they behave according to their assigned label.

Behavior determines identity, and if people are no longer abusing drugs and alcohol they should adopt a new identity. In contrast, many self-help groups reinforce a lifelong addiction identity by reminding people of the addiction experience while accusing those who object to this negative self-labeling as being in denial. This kind of labeling is actually counterproductive to recovery. Labeling is reinforced by some treatment providers who medicalize behavior by calling it a disease (see chapter 4), which implies a passive approach to treatment as well as a sense of helplessness in addiction. Addiction is thought to be a lifelong disease for which there is no cure. The addict is encouraged to manage his disease by total abstinence, lifelong participation in AA, and acceptance of the Twelve Steps theory of addiction. The Twelve Steps theory of addiction treatment misapplies a religious determinism to addiction behavior by implying that people cannot choose to behave differently. In contrast, biblical theology suggests the opposite, which is that behavior determines identity. For example, Paul tells the Corinthian Christians that drunkards will not inherit the kingdom of God (1 Corinthians 6:9), but then he says, "And that is what some of you were" (v. 11). Could he say this if they had continued their past behaviors? No, because then they would be excluded from the kingdom of God. Drunkenness is described as one of the "acts of the sinful nature" (Galatians 5:19) and "those who live like this will not inherit the kingdom of God" (v. 21). Notice that the emphasis in Scripture is on acting and living as the basis of personal identity.

When I run addiction groups I never encourage people to repeat negative statements about themselves unless it describes current or planned behavior. If people are not now engaging in the behavior and have no plans to do so in the future, then it is better for them to state positive things about themselves. For example, one could say, "I once was addicted to alcohol, but now I am acting more responsibly." Or, "I no longer see myself as a drug addict because I have other things in my life that I would rather do." Addiction identity is a fundamental flaw of the Twelve Steps theory, disease model, and AA approach to addiction treatment. The self-help and therapy groups that engage in the long-term self-labeling process of addiction identity encourage a sense of powerlessness and helplessness regarding addiction.

Personal identity, or how people view themselves, is a crucial element in what is called natural recovery. Natural recovery occurs when people recover from long-term drug and alcohol abuse on their own and without outside intervention. Research by Granfield and Cloud (1996) suggests that negative self-labeling is a major obstacle to natural recovery. Granfield and Cloud interviewed a large number of these people and found that the defining characteristic of the natural recovery group was their refusal to adopt an addiction identity, "The fact that our respondents did not adopt addict identities is of great importance since it contradicts the common assumptions of treatment programs" (51). Another key aspect of natural recovery that researchers found is the rejection of powerlessness, "Consequently, these respondents found the suggestion that they were powerless incompatible with their own self-image" (53). What this research shows is the damaging impact the addiction label and identity can have on recovery.

Trapped Like Rats

Perhaps one of the most significant experiments ever conducted in the field of drug addiction is by psychologist Bruce Alexander and colleagues (1980). Alexander was interested to know if environmental factors were a better predictor of opiate consumption than other factors, such as drug availability and the addictive power of the drug. The idea for the experiment came from a university seminar he attended on coping with addiction. One individual at this seminar insisted that environment had little to do with addiction and that addiction was because of humankind's natural affinity for drugs. For support of his argument, the individual cited experiments of drug consumption conducted on animals in laboratories. It was thought that this proved the power of the drug since laboratory conditions would eliminate the environmental problems the animals faced in their natural environments. Alexander was not convinced of this, and he thought the laboratory environment was actually causing the rats to consume drugs. Since no experimentation had been done in this area, he and his colleagues decided to set up a much better environment, called the Rat Park, that would give rats the freedom to do the things rats love to do. For comparison, other rats were placed in cages under normal laboratory conditions. This became known as the great Rat Park experiment.

For more than four years, a series of experiments were conducted with rats living under these two conditions. The goal of the experiment was to learn whether animals consumed drugs because of a natural affinity or because of what Alexander believed to be stressful laboratory conditions. One group of rats was isolated in small individual cages such as would be normally found in a laboratory environment. The second group was housed together in a spacious environment that provided opportunities for socialization and play. Two drinkable liquids were provided for the rats in both environments. Although both liquids tasted identical, one contained morphine and the other did not. Results of the first test showed that rats in both environments preferred the drink without morphine. The authors then hooked the rats on morphine for 57 days, which allowed plenty of time to form an addiction, and then allowed them a choice once again:

> ...we proceeded to the "Seduction" and "Kicking-the-habit" experiments. In them, the environmental effects were crystal clear. No matter how much we induced, seduced, or tempted them, the Rat Park rats resisted drinking the narcotic solution. The caged rats drank plenty, however, ranging up to *16 times* as much as the Rat Park residents in one experimental phase, and measuring 10 times as much in some other phases. (56)

Since rats cannot be interviewed, it is not possible to know exactly why the Rat Park rats did so well, but the researchers theorize it is because the anesthetic and tranquilizer effect of the drug interfered with the pleasurable activities of play, eating, sex, and socialization that the Rat Park rats enjoyed. In other words, the rats valued other things more than the effect of the drug. Alexander argues that humans are a lot like rats. If you put humans in stressful conditions, they are more vulnerable to opiate drugs than under other conditions. Perhaps this explains why 90 per cent of heroin addicted soldiers in Vietnam were able to kick the habit when they returned home, or why most who use opiates in the hospital do not crave these drugs when they get well.

This is an excellent article and seems to support the argument that both environment and values play a larger role in addiction than the power of the drugs themselves. This experiment also calls in question certain assumptions in our current national war on illegal drugs; that is, it may not be the drugs but what is going on in people's lives that cause them to become addicts. A valuable lesson from this research is that if we want to understand addiction, we should first try "to perceive the dimensions of our own cages as clearly as we see those which house the rats" (56).

So, the cause of addiction is not drugs but the failure of people to adequately cope with their strong feelings about the way they perceive themselves and their environments. Examples of the failure to cope with negative feelings is often seen in love songs written by musicians. Song writers can be more in touch with the realities and frustrations of living than the mental health community. As an example, notice the words of a song by country music singer John Michael Montgomery:

> I ain't nothin' but beer and bones
> Honey since I lost you
> I ain't ate a bite
> Since the night
> That you said we're through
> Got to work this morning
> Early this afternoon
> Yeah my boss man nudged me
> Said son I need to talk to you
> You used to make me money
> But lately I been taking a loss
> Well he smelled my breath
> Gave me what was left

Of the day off

Many would look at the story in this song and blame the man's alcohol abuse on genes, disease, brainwaves, serotonin levels, or some other biological explanation. This must be the answer, they reason, for why else would someone embark on such a downward spiral? But this completely ignores what is obviously portrayed in the song, and in this case, the song writer is more perceptive that the therapist. It is not beer, or the alcohol in beer, but the loss of a love relationship that motivates the character in the song to stay drunk. Peele (2004) argues that addiction "is nearly always tied to relationship problems, to the absence of or search for intimacy and companionship" (114). The man in the song is not coping effectively with his strong feelings over the loss of a love relationship and he is using alcohol as a way to cope with this loss. Rather than deal with these negative feelings, he continues to engage in behavior that harms himself and perhaps others. If people do not adequately cope with their feelings about relationships and love, they can develop many of the harmful characteristics of a mental disorder; that is, with some people, love can be a form of craziness. As the song suggests, people often turn to alcohol as a way of coping with the strong feelings they have regarding a lost relationship. All kinds of addiction, including drugs, alcohol, gambling, risky sex, violence, and compulsive shopping are inappropriate responses to perceived unhappiness.

This is not to suggest that losing a love relationship is not hurtful, but there are better ways of dealing with it than drug or alcohol addiction. There is no doubt that people sometimes experience the dimensions of their own cages, but humans are not rats, and people can make adjustments to the kinds of responses they make to bad events. Many young men turned to heroin when they were sent to Viet Nam, which is understandable because they were in a very stressful environment and the drug was readily available, but many other young men experienced the same stressful environment without turning to heroin. Likewise, men and women lose the relationship of a significant other every day without inappropriately turning to drugs and alcohol as a way to escape from their strong feelings. The statement, "I cannot live without love," is false because many people do live without love. Others survive broken relationships and go on to live productive lives and some even find better relationships.

Addiction Myths

1. Addiction is a disease. Addiction is a behavior, and about the only place in the world where behavior is thought of as a disease is in the United States of America. Although other approaches are gaining ground, the disease model is still the dominant view in this country. Eventually, more practical cognitive approaches will replace the disease model and the Twelve Steps theory of treatment. Cognitive approaches believe that addiction is a choice (Schaler, 2000) and treatment focuses on people's belief about themselves and their environments. Many cognitive approaches use an appraisal process in which addicts weigh the costs and benefits of their continuing addiction. Recent examples of this approach are Miller (2002) and Peele (2004).

2. The disease model approach to treatment works. It would be more accurate to say that the disease model approach to treatment does not work. George Vaillant (1983), a proponent and leading authority on the disease model, says, "there is compelling evidence that the results of our treatment were no better than the natural history of the disease" (284). Unfortunately, the failure of the disease model treatment approach only reinforces the belief in the minds of many that alcohol addiction is a biological disease. The disease model is actually counter productive in that it instills in people the false belief that they are sick instead of behaving badly. It also encourages people to believe they are helpless and cannot control their behavior.

3. Gateway drugs. A gateway drug is said to naturally lead the user to supposedly more dangerous drugs. To frighten people away from certain illegal drugs, for example, marijuana, the argument is often made that marijuana use leads to heroin use. What these drugs have in common, however, is the personality of the user and not some mysterious connection. It would be just as ridiculous to argue that nicotine and alcohol are gateway drugs to gambling. In Las Vegas, the casinos resist nicotine restrictions and bring alcohol drinks to gamblers because people who consume large amounts of nicotine and alcohol also tend to gamble large amounts of money. The reason they do this is because of the similarities of people's personalities and values and not because of some biological connection between drugs and gambling. In defense of the gateway concept, the argument is made that statistics show that people experiment with marijuana before they consume heroin. This may be true, but statistics also show that most people smoke marijuana after they have smoked nicotine, and there is a statistical relationship between drinking coffee and smoking cigarettes. So, is caffeine a gateway drug to heroin?

4. You cannot understand addiction unless you have been there. I usually get this from clients who think that unless I have been addicted to their particular drug I do not know how to help them stop their addictions. I am not sure how being an expert in messing up your life qualifies you to be an addictions counselor, but this is a myth that is believed and accepted by many. This same argument could be applied to every kind of addiction and it would be impossible for therapists to have personal experience with every conceivable kind of addiction or behavior. There is no empirical evidence to suggest that personal experience with an addiction helps in the treatment of others. A good reason not to answer a question like this is that it is impossible to answer without doing some harm. Regardless of which way you answer, the client now feels differently about you as a counselor, and it is unlikely your response is helpful to the client.

5. Drugs cause behavior. I heard a news report about a young man who was arrested for breaking in several businesses to steal what he could find. The news reporter said, "His parents blame a cocaine addiction for his behavior." Drugs may lower inhibitions, or cause us to feel powerful and euphoric, but they do not force us to behave in certain ways. The idea of involuntary behavior is a myth. People take drugs because they want to, and sometimes the drugs give them the courage to act in ways they would not when they are sober, but the decision to act is always in the individual's power to make. It is also false to suggest that drugs cause addiction. People cause addiction because addiction is a behavior. Drugs do not cause addiction any more than guns kill people or SUVs run over pedestrians; yet, these myths continue to exist in our culture and these beliefs are often written in newspaper headlines.

The idea of blaming others, or even non-living objects, for our behavior is as old as the Garden of Eden. Adam told God that it was "the woman you put here with me" (Genesis 3:12) that caused him to eat of the fruit. When Moses confronted Aaron about the golden calf,

Aaron said the people gave him their gold and "I threw it into the fire, and out came this calf!" (Exodus 32:24). This is the same kind of logic employed by many addicts to justify their irresponsible behaviors. Many in the treatment field encourage this kind of thinking when they argue that addicts are helpless and powerless in the face of addiction. People made the golden calf just like people take drugs. An attribution error occurs when we falsely attribute behaviors to non-living substances like gold and drugs. An error in reasoning occurs when people focus on the object of the addiction rather than the behavior, as in a public service announcement I heard recently, "Nicotine may be addictive to some people." The impression given is that this drug is dangerous because some people do not have any control over its power. No drug has the power to suddenly take over your life. I know this goes against conventional wisdom and the myths regarding the supposed overwhelming power of drugs, but the focus in the public service announcement is on the wrong thing and it is a misunderstanding of the nature of addiction.

6. *I take drugs and gamble because I want to be free.* Many people are under the illusion that they are expressing their freedoms when they give in to compulsions, but the opposite occurs because people lose their freedoms to addictions. All one has to do is visit the prison system to understand how confining drugs and alcohol can be or just observe a nicotine addict desperately searching for a place where he can legally smoke a cigarette. Addiction, like sin, gives the illusion of freedom, but Jesus said, "everyone who sins is a slave to sin" (John 8:34). Paul rightly asks, "Don't you know that when you offer yourselves to someone to obey him as slaves, you are slaves to the one whom you obey—whether you are slaves to sin, which leads to death, or to obedience, which leads to righteousness?" (Romans 6:16). There is a saying, "Only he that is tied to chart and compass has freedom of the seas." Likewise, only those who control their behaviors are masters of their world.

Helping Others Change

How do you get someone to change? Do you force them? Preach to them? Persuade them? Counsel them? People should be given the freedom to live their lives as they please as long as they do not harm others. I fear that if society forces people to change simply because they hold unconventional values, then society may try to force me to give up something that I value that others do not. Change, therefore, must be voluntary and we should not force people to change self-destructive behaviors or incarcerate them simply because they choose to ruin their lives in the pursuit of addictions. For real change to occur, people must come to the conclusion that it is in their own best interest to change.

For those who believe in a biblical moral standard for their lives, the Bible can be a very useful tool in preventing and stopping addiction. Although preaching and counseling are not the same, there can be therapeutic value in both, and what both should have in common is the pursuit of voluntary change.

Biblical preaching is the attempt to persuade people to conform their lives to the moral standard of the Bible. In evangelism, an example would be Luke's account of Paul's preaching at Ephesus, "Paul entered the synagogue and spoke boldly there for three months, arguing persuasively about the kingdom of God" (Acts 19:8). Note that Paul was trying to persuade the people rather than force them to believe.

Preaching can be a tool that God uses to change people's hearts and lives for the better. Through preaching, the Bible says that God is "at work in you who believe" (1 Thessalonians 2:13). God will work in your life, but he will not do it all. There is no easy button religion. The hearer has an obligation to make the necessary application to life, "Do not merely listen to the word, and so deceive yourselves. Do what it says" (James 1:22). Preaching is not forcing or intimidating others to do what they do not want to do, it is simply making the case for change. The Bible nowhere suggests that Christians are to make converts at the point of a sword, or force people to conform to the teaching of Christ. Biblical evangelism was never a Christian jihad waged against unbelievers. For example, when Paul gives instructions about disciplining those in the church, he does not apply this to those who do not believe (1 Corinthians 5:9-11). So, if people choose not to accept the values of the gospel, they should be free to reject the message. In the same manner, just as preachers have the right to preach, society has a right to present a consensus message to the public about the use and misuse of drugs. This does not mean that all people listen to the message. There is always a small portion of society that chooses to pursue drug abuse behavior. So then, why do some people choose to ignore the messages of the majority culture regarding the use and misuse of drugs? It is because they do not share the values of the majority who seek to restrict the behavior of the minority. In our society, we go a step further by attempting to force people to conform to drug laws, and if they do not conform to these laws they can be sent to prison. Laws against driving under the influence of drugs are practical because they attempt to protect the innocent. Laws against individual possession and use of certain drugs are intended to force people to conform to what society feels is in everyone's own best interest, which is a judgment call that society has made about certain kinds of behaviors.

In biblical preaching, the goal is to use the message of the Bible to work on people's hearts. This is why preaching should be biblically based because the power for change is in the word of God and not in the advice of the preacher. According to Paul, the gospel is "the power of God for the salvation of everyone who believes" (Romans 1:16). Most people today think of preaching in a negative way, as in, "Don't preach to me!" This negative perception of preaching is really not what biblical preaching is about. Instead, it is a tool that God uses to bring about growth and change to those who believe, or to persuade those who do not believe. Preaching is a part of God's design for the church, which is why the Bible says there are evangelists and preaching elders (Ephesians 4:11; 1 Timothy 5:17). The job of these servants is to build up the body of Christ through biblical preaching (Myers, 2003). For religious people who are biblically focused, preaching can be a positive tool in the prevention of drug and alcohol abuse. As Miller (1998) argues, alcohol and drug problems are often associated with an absence of faith and religion, but the therapeutic value of religion assumes that people are actually *involved* in their religion (Levin, 2001). As beneficial as religion can be in both preventing and stopping addiction, it is not a requirement for change because people have already been endowed by their creator with the ability to make choices about their behaviors.

A New Identity

Stanton Peele (2004) points out that addicts tend to have a negative outlook on life because "they experience life as a series of problems that they are unable to cope with" (111). A primary characteristic of these people is that they have an external locus of control when it comes to addiction; that is, they allow outside events to control their behaviors. They falsely believe they cannot cope with their problems without drugs. This negative outlook becomes a self-fulfilling prophecy as they panic or feel depressed when they experience negative feelings or difficult circumstances. There is also the inertia following an initial misstep that keeps addicts in the addiction rut. Peele gives a good example of this kind of thinking and action:

> I once attended an alcohol support group where a woman described how a series of quick decisions ruined her life. Although she had not had a drink in six years, she ended up at a bar. She had a drink. She drank too much and became drunk. She got in her car and drove. She was stopped by the police and arrested. She lost her license. Unable to drive, she lost her job. Her husband then divorced her.

> This woman portrayed her eventual decline as the inevitable result of her first misstep. But the truth is that at any point she could have exited from the cascade of disasters. She could, of course, have avoided the bar. She could have sat at the bar but had a soft drink. She could have gone to the bar, had one drink, and then gone home. She could even have gotten drunk but then taken a cab home from the bar. She could have developed an alternative transportation plan to get herself to work. (121)

As people journey down the road of addiction they get caught up in a downward spiral of events, or what Peele calls a cascade of disasters. Why is it that some people seem helpless to make the necessary corrections to these negative life events? More than anything else, I believe the answer to this question lies in the addiction identity. Unfortunately, this negative addiction identity is the very thing that is promoted in many treatment programs.

A key to change, therefore, is to get a new identity. As we learned earlier in this chapter, behavior should determine personal identity and not the other way around. Behavior flows naturally from our beliefs and values, and it is our beliefs, values, and behavior that determine who we are. Let us now consider how to lose an addiction identity and form a new one.

Through a cognitive appraisal process, people can sort out the pros and cons of their present addiction behavior so that they can discover what is in their own best interest. For example, people can list all of the negative aspects of their addiction as well as the positive aspects. They can also list the negative and positive long-term aspects of addiction.

Since the focus of most thinking about addictions is on immediate gratification, a crucial part of this appraisal process is the listing of the long-term negative consequences of addiction. There are really no long-term benefits of addiction, so to change their beliefs, people must be convinced that long-term gratification can actually be more beneficial to them than the short-term gratification of their addiction. Although other short-term gratifications can be found to substitute for the present addiction, most addicts prefer and value their current addiction over other short-term gratification replacements. This is why it is essential that people develop a new awareness of and belief in the value of long-term gratification. When this happens, a new set of values form about what people really want out of life. These new values cause them to reassess their current behaviors. People can learn, for example, to value relationships, work, health, children, education, and personal integrity more than their addictions by focusing on a long-term view of their lives. To get to this point, individuals may have to change from their present worldly focus by having some kind of spiritual experience; that is, they must be able to stand outside of themselves and view their lives more objectively (see chapter 2).

There are many things people can value that have positive long-term benefits. Eating well, exercise, and pursuing a healthy lifestyle have positive long-term benefits and lead to increased self-esteem. Getting a job and being successful at work, as well as providing for one's family and gaining a measure of material success are things to be valued. Going to church, having a relationship with God, and growing in the knowledge of the Bible are things that can be valued by religious people. Hearing biblical sermons and being encouraged by other Christians can prevent relapse and strengthen the will. People can also learn to value their integrity and good name. The Bible says, "A good name is more desirable than great riches; to be esteemed is better than silver or gold" (Proverbs 22:1).

A new identity strengthens the will and overcomes temptation. I knew a man once who turned his life around by saying, "This is not who I want to be." He was having an identity crisis until he realized who he wanted to be. The woman in Stanton Peele's story abused alcohol because she did not know who she was when she first noticed the bar. Going in the bar was not her downfall; rather, it was her indecision about who she was, or perhaps her own addiction identity, that led her to the cascade of disasters. Had she developed a non-addiction identity, her responses would have been different. For example, when she saw the bar, she could have said something like this to herself, "I see that bar over there but there is really nothing there for me now because I no longer abuse alcohol." Had she gone in the bar, she could have said, "I think I will have a soft drink instead of a beer because it is not in my own best interest to be consuming alcohol in this place." Had she had a beer instead, she could have said, "One beer is enough because I do not want to go into some altered state of consciousness by abusing alcohol tonight." And so it goes with each circumstance, a strong identity determines the kind of response that prevents a downward spiral of events.

There is a story in the Bible of a young man named Daniel who was taken in captivity by the Babylonians. Daniel and his friends were probably in their teens when they were taken away from their homes and taught the ways of the Babylonians in the great city of Babylon. Daniel is one of the few men in the Bible of which there is nothing bad said about his life. He is like Nathanael in the New Testament, of whom Jesus said, "Here is a true Israelite, in whom there is nothing false" (John 1:47). How could Daniel have had so much strength and integrity at such a young age? How could Daniel be so diligent about maintaining his Jewish culture and religious faith while being in such an environment? I believe the answer to this is found in Daniel's strong personal identity that is revealed near the beginning of the story, "But Daniel resolved not to defile himself..." (Daniel 1:8). It does not say when Daniel made this decision, but I suspect he made it well before he ever got to Babylon. The key to changing a behavior is deciding what you are going to do before you make a decision, and if this is done, then the decision is much easier to make. The woman in Peele's story illustrates what happens when you do not decide things until you are exposed to the temptation. Perhaps she was ambivalent in her feelings about alcohol, or she did not have a strong non-addiction identity, but when she first saw the bar she was not certain about who she was at that moment. Her mistake was to approach the bar with confusion about her identity, and when she did, her addiction identity took over and governed her every decision for the rest of the night.

A good way to reinforce a new identity is to verbalize it, as Carlo DiClemente (2003) recommends in his book, *Addiction and Change*. For example, addicts who seek change should complete the following sentences: 1) The changes I want to make are…2) The most important reasons why I want to make these changes are…3) The steps I plan to take in changing are…4) I will know if my plan is working if…(159). Notice how this parallels what Jesus asked of people who wanted change: "Do you want to be healed?…What do you want me to do?" (see chapter 8).

If you want to maintain a new identity you have to remember who you are. Most people do this naturally and their own personal identity governs their lives, but recovering addicts are often confused about their identity due to their own ambivalence as well as the mixed signals coming from the media, treatment providers, and self-help groups.

It is possible for people to adopt a new identity and biblical teaching suggests it was a part of the Christian experience. For example, Paul reminded the Christians at Colosse, "You used to walk in these ways, in the life you once lived" (Colossians 3:7). He goes on to say that you cannot lie to one another any more "since you have taken off the old self with its practices and have put on the new self" (vs. 9-10). The lesson here is that people can change their behaviors by taking on the new Christian identity. Paul makes no allowances for those who have a lying disease, or lying genes, but he does feel that they need an occasional reminder about their new identity in case they forget who they are. A lapse does not become a relapse if there is a strong personal identity to go back to, and once people contemplate what they have done in lapsing, they can say to themselves, "This is not who I am."

Conclusion

By labeling people it is possible to assign them an identity that discourages change. When people repeat negative and self-defeating statements about themselves and their addictions, it reinforces the addiction identity as well as the behavior. Instead of assigning labels, it is far better to encourage people to change their identities by changing their behaviors. People tend to resist relapse if they establish a non-addiction identity prior to experiencing a circumstance that might encourage them to engage in their addictions. It is important to first change your beliefs and then establish a new set of values because it is from our beliefs and values that behavior flows.

Recommended Reading

To contemplate change, we must first have some idea about the nature of addiction. One of the best overall views of the drug and alcohol addiction problem is *Drugs: Should we Legalize, Decriminalize or Deregulate?* edited by Jeffrey Schaler (1998). Although this book focuses on issues surrounding drugs and alcohol, there are common threads found among all addictions. This book is also important because it provides an easy way to access the "The Rat Park Chronicle" article by Bruce Alexander and colleagues that first appeared in the *British Columbia Medical Journal* in 1980. Alexander's animal experiment is one of the more important studies ever conducted in this field of study and it is a shame that his research has not been used more than it has. Another must read article in this book is the one by Lee N. Robins and colleagues on returning Vietnam veterans and heroin use. Most heroin addicted soldiers returning from Vietnam were able to stop because they left a stressful environment and once they returned home, they found other things they valued more than their continuing addictions. Schaler has also put together several articles by various authors who give a balanced presentation of the arguments for and against the decriminalization of drugs. If you have never given this issue much thought, read these articles so that you can be better informed of the arguments on both sides. Finally, read the entire section of the book titled, "Addiction is a Behavior: The Myth of Loss of Control."

Questions for Discussion

1. Why should behavior determine identity? What is the danger in labeling people?

2. What is the lesson learned from the Rat Park experiment? What does this say about addiction?

3. What are the addiction myths listed in this chapter? Can you think of others? Are there any myths in the list that you feel are true? If so, why?

4. How can we help someone who is addicted? Is it possible to help someone who will not help themselves? When does helping become enabling?

5. Why is it beneficial to have a non-addiction identity before one experiences the opportunity to engage in an addiction?

6. Discuss the saying: "Only he that is tied to chart and compass has freedom of the seas." How is it possible for one to find freedom in self-discipline?

Chapter 8
How to Change

Knowing is Half the Battle

When my three sons were little boys, they watched a cartoon program called G. I. Joe on Saturday mornings. Sometimes they begged me to watch it with them and we would lie down on the floor together and watch the show. Mixed among the advertisements for each show was a G. I. Joe public service announcement. The cartoon character had some beneficial statement for the children in the audience, for example, "Look both ways before crossing a street." Following each public service announcement, G. I. Joe would say to the children, "And now you know, and knowing is half the battle." I often use this example in counseling because it stresses the importance of knowledge.

Knowledge is empowering, and the more people know about their addictions, the easier it is for them to change their behaviors. Knowledge also casts out fear. Many people do not understand what has led to their dependencies or the nature of their addictions and, as a result, they are afraid of their own feelings and desires. Or, they are afraid because they have tried to quit in the past and failed, or they do not know how to quit. All of these fears, however, lead to inaction and helplessness. Let me illustrate by giving an example from sports. When I was in high school, we were scheduled to play a large high school that had a good team. The team began running a play against our zone defense that was working every time. The coach called a timeout, and as I walked back to the huddle I felt discouraged and defeated because I had no idea how to keep them from scoring against our defense. The coach told us about an adjustment we could make that would stop the play they were running. As I left the huddle I felt completely different about our prospects for success because now I knew something to do. When we returned to the game we made the adjustment and it worked. Had it not worked, the coach probably would have told us another way to adjust to their offense, but just knowing how to make an adjustment to our defense gave me a whole new perspective on the game that day. For me, knowing was half the battle, and now all I had to do was go out and implement the plan.

Knowing is half the battle because knowledge can remove the false beliefs that keep people in the addiction rut. For example, if people believe they are physically addicted to alcohol and cannot survive without it, it is unlikely they will stop abusing alcohol because they believe their behavior is predestined and out of control (Marlatt & Gordon, 1985). Aaron Beck (1993) has noted a common thread of false beliefs across various types of addictions (cocaine, opiates, alcohol, nicotine, and prescription drugs) as well as other kinds of destructive behaviors, such as binge eating. These false beliefs can serve as "the groundwork for relapse" (38). So, if you change your beliefs, you can change your behaviors. Knowledge is the key to changing beliefs, which is why knowing is half the battle.

What is it that people should know about addiction to make a change? First, people need to realize that addiction produces strong feelings, and these intense feelings can discourage them from making a change. Giving in to feelings and urges simply because they are strong perpetuates problem behavior. The fact that we experience strong feelings is natural and a part of living, so people cannot assume defeat every time they experience these feelings. Second, people need to understand the reasons for their own behaviors. For example, people may abuse drugs and alcohol because of any or all of the following reasons: what they model, an attempt to escape some unpleasant memory, the experience of a broken relationship, or unhappiness with something in their environment. This information can be useful in learning how to cope with feelings. Knowledge about the motivations for behavior can help people view their behavior more objectively and perhaps discover possible solutions. Stanton Peele (2004) argues that the rewards of addiction sometimes disappear if they are identified for what they are; in other words, when people explain to themselves why they pursue certain gratifications, they can remove the power of their attraction. Peele argues that this "may allow you to put your finger on something you know is not right or needs to be changed" (93), which is why knowing is half the battle.

When people are chemically dependent and experience physical withdrawal because of prolonged drug use, they need to understand what is taking place in their bodies and why they are experiencing these symptoms. Knowledge reduces anxiety, and if people know that withdrawal symptoms naturally occur because the body is adjusting to life without these chemicals, then they will be encouraged to endure the discomfort of withdrawal, but if they believe physical withdrawal means they cannot live without drugs, they will never quit.

Understand Gratification

Some people never seem to understand gratification, or if they do, they ignore the principle. The laws of gratification became apparent to me at a very early age. I was perhaps 4 or 5 years old when my brother and I would ride to the grocery store with my mother. As a treat, she would give each of us a dime to spend as we pleased. At the time, one of my favorite treats was an ice cream sandwich that consisted of vanilla ice cream between two chocolate wafers. My older brother told me he was going to save his dimes for a toy he wanted. I wanted that toy too but I also wanted the ice cream sandwich. So, this was my first encounter with the laws of gratification; that is, should I enjoy the immediate gratification of the ice cream sandwich or do I exchange the present gratification for a future benefit that I might enjoy even more. I weighed the rewards in my mind—sandwich now, toy later—and then I made my choice. I chose the sandwich, which means I also chose to give up the long-term gratification of getting a toy. A few weeks later, my brother had enough dimes to purchase his toy. Although I also wanted the same toy and thought about whining to my mother about it, I felt there was something wrong about whining when I knew all along that I would have to give up the toy if I chose the ice cream sandwich. Immediate gratification is not always wrong, and there was nothing wrong with me choosing the ice cream sandwich over the toy. I actually wanted the toy more than the sandwich but I did not want it enough to wait for it, which means that waiting made the toy less valuable to me. The point is not that we choose immediate gratification, but that we recognize what the choice entails. If we think about it, the cost of forfeiting a future benefit may become more important to us than the immediate gratification we desire now. As long as we are making a rational choice, we always know what to do that is our own best interest.

Some may think the mental processes of a child are not great enough to make these kinds of calculations, but I remember clearly what was going through my mind at the time. Perhaps we make gratification more complex than it really is by looking for the cause of addiction in brainwaves, genes, parents, society, disease, and environment. What we are talking about is not really complicated. The point is this: immediate gratification usually entails the forfeiture of a long-term gratification. Gratification itself, whether short-term or long-term, is neither good nor bad. Some gratification, however, may not be in our own best interest, and for those who are religious, it may even be sinful. The key is to get people to become more spiritual when they consider gratification; that is, they should try to stand outside of themselves and take a more objective look at their decisions and choices.

This reminds me of the time my youngest son, Jared, graduated from high school. I explained to my son that he now had two choices before him regarding his future. Should he go to college or should he get a full-time job and begin a career? I emphasized that it was his decision to make and that I would love him regardless of what decision he made. I explained that although many young people do not go to college and still succeed in life, there are some advantages in getting a college degree. I also explained that there would be some short-term and long-term gratification issues he would have to sort through in making this decision. On the one hand, if he got a job now, he could start enjoying the benefits of having a regular income. He would be in a position to live independently from his parents and buy a nice vehicle to drive. On the other hand, if he went to college, he must endure four years of hard work and self-denial, but in the end he would have a college degree that would stay with him for the rest of his life. In addition, his choice of a major field of study was also based on the laws of gratification. He chose to major in computer science rather than some other field of study that he might also enjoy. Computer science was a difficult field of study and there were no guarantees he would even be able to complete it. Jared had many interests and he could have studied many other things that would have been easier for him than computer science, but he chose computer science because of his long-term goal of having a skill that would be both practical and marketable in the present age. So, after four years of hard work and self-denial, Jared was able to graduate with a degree in computer science and now has a professional job in his field of study.

The laws of gratification are crucial in understanding why some people choose addiction and others do not. The problem with addiction is that people tend to have a worldly focus rather than a spiritual focus (see chapter 2), and their focus is always fixed on the present with little or no thought for the future. With a worldly focus, people neglect to consider the long-term damaging aspects of their behaviors. In Scripture, the laws of gratification can be compared to God's law of harvest, which is, "A man reaps what he sows" (Galatians 6:7). The law of harvest also includes the promise of a long-term benefit, "Let us not become weary in doing good, for at the proper time we will reap a harvest if we do not give up" (v. 9). The problem with addicts is that they want to reap the harvest of gratification now rather than later. This mindset is the result of a long history of decision-making based on a worldly focus. The longer people follow this course in life the more difficult it is for them to stop their addiction.

So, how do you help someone change from a worldly focus to a spiritual focus? How do you help them get out of the rut of addiction? If they are open to receiving help, suggest that they try to find a substitute gratification for the one that is causing problems. It is unlikely they will find a substitute that is as gratifying as what they are now experiencing, but the idea is to help them transition away from a harmful behavior by replacing it with one that is less harmful. Second, practice harm reduction. For example, nicotine addicts may try to find a less harmful way to ingest the drug other than by smoking, or they can reduce the number of cigarettes smoked in a given time period. Third, use cognitive restructuring (see chapter 5) to help people change their beliefs about their addictive behaviors. They must recognize that the long-term negative consequences of addiction are more harmful than the benefits of the immediate gratification. It is surprising how many people never really do a cognitive appraisal and count the cost of addiction. It is like the problem gambler who only remembers the wins and not the losses or fails to understand the laws of probability. However, when people discover that addiction is not in their own best interest, they often find the motivation to stop. Fourth, reframe the benefits of addiction in negative ways. This requires monitoring your self-talk. When you say to yourself, "Boy, I sure would like to drink/gamble/smoke," respond by saying, "I know what this will do to me and it is not good." Finally, there is a certain satisfaction in waiting to receive a long-term gratification, as in the saying, "wanting is half of having." Waiting all week to go to a nice restaurant makes the actual experience more gratifying. There can actually be pleasure in denying yourself an immediate gratification if you know it leads to a more important gratification later.

If it is as simple as is suggested above, then why do people not stop their addictions? It is not that they are unable to, but the pain of quitting and the sudden loss of gratification is something they do not want to experience. This creates a significant resistance to change even though they may be aware that in the long-term it is in their own best interest to stop their present behavior. Another problem is that many people cannot find a substitute gratification that helps them transition from drugs, alcohol, or gambling. Finally, while most people value long-term gratification, addicts often do not.

Get Out of the Rut

People get in the rut of addiction and it is hard for them to break out. When I was a young boy, we used to have an old Ford pickup that I would drive around on the dirt roads where we lived. In the winter, when there was a lot of rain, the ruts in the roads would get very deep. They were so bad sometimes that once you got in the ruts you could not easily get out. In fact, the truck would almost steer itself because of the deep ruts; that is, if I let go of the steering wheel, the ruts would take control of the truck. When we start down the road of life, sometimes we get ourselves in ruts that are so deep that it is almost impossible to get out.

This reminds me of a story that my friend, Lonnie Davis, told me when he was a young preacher. It seems that he and the song leader were good friends and they were always joking with each other. One Sunday before worship services began, Lonnie asked the song leader about his first song for the worship hour. As they were looking at the song, Lonnie began to sing the song off key and to a different tune. Well, they had a big laugh about how silly it sounded, but when the song leader stood up to lead his first song he could not get the silly tune out of his mind. Every time he tried to lead the song he led the wrong tune! The silly tune put him in a rut and he could not get out. Addicts play the same addiction tune over and over in their heads, and the longer they travel down the addiction path the deeper the ruts get. The farther down the addiction road you travel the harder it is to stop, turn around, and go back the other way. Let us now consider some ways to get out of the rut and go in the right direction.

1. *Do you want to get well?* Not everyone is willing to endure the pain and sacrifice to get out of the addiction rut. To make a major change like this, people have to be highly motivated. A spouse, counselors, friends, and parents may not recognize that the real problem is not the addiction but the lack of desire to change. Without a strong desire to change, intervention strategies are useless. Addicts may not even recognize their own lack of desire for change, and so introspection is necessary before change occurs.

The Bible tells the story of a healing that Jesus did in Jerusalem at a pool called Bethesda. There was a man there who had been disabled for 38 years. When Jesus observed his condition, he asked the man, "Do you want to get well?" (John 5:6). On the surface, this question seems out of place, irrelevant, and even nonsensical. Would not everyone want to be healed of a disability? I believe, however, that all of Jesus' questions had a point, and I also believe this question had some relevance to the man's condition. The man had been disabled for 38 years, and if he were to be healed, his whole world would change. For example, he would have to live differently, get a job, learn not to be dependent on others, and make a dramatic change in his lifestyle. Now, most people would readily accept these challenges if they could get well, but there are some people who are ambivalent about getting well. In some ways they may want to get well, but they may also want to stay in the rut because of the pain required to get out. As they contemplate the difficulty of change, they may view their life in the rut more favorably. To illustrate, consider Joe, a man who has abused alcohol for many years. As Joe is being slowly consumed by his addiction, he takes on less and less responsibility for his life. He has accepted the sickness label and the addiction identity. His children make allowances for his behavior because they have been told he has a disease. His wife manages the family finances, pays the bills, and allows Joe an allowance for his drinking. She now supports the family with her job, disciplines the children, and makes all the major decisions in the household. Joe stays home, baby sits the children, and drinks. Joe may say he wants to get well, but does he really? Notice the major changes he would have to make in his life. Joe has gotten comfortable in his addiction lifestyle and he may not want to change because it involves self-denial, pain, energy, and new responsibilities. Right now, Joe is in a comfortable addiction rut because his wife enables him in his addiction.

2. Expect resistance. Inertia is the resistance to change. When I was young, I used to move large sacks of hog feed by placing them in a wheelbarrow. The problem, however, was getting the wheelbarrow started after I put the load in. An enormous amount of energy was required to get it moving, but once moving, the load was much easier to handle than having to carry the load. If the least obstacle, such as a small stone, were in front of the wheel of the wheelbarrow, it made the resistance even worse. Likewise, the biggest challenge people have in changing the direction of their lives is getting started. Even small obstacles, like the little stones in front of the wheelbarrow, can create enormous resistance when people first try to change their behavior. Addicts often believe that resistance will always be this hard and perhaps even harder, but this is not the case. When change has begun, just like the wheelbarrow as it begins to roll, the burden becomes easier to bear. Getting started is always the hardest part of change. So, the challenge for most addicts is to stop contemplating the difficulty and begin the change that leads to a better life.

3. Take the initiative in treatment. Many people who are stuck in the addiction rut are not aggressive in seeking change and become passive in their treatment. Many addicts assume a sickness identity, often encouraged by their enablers and treatment professionals, and they start depending on others to create change in their lives. So, take the initiative in finding your own way out of the rut.

4. Articulate your needs. If you do not know where you are going, it is unlikely you will ever get there. If you want to make a change, formulate and then verbalize your goals so that you can know where you are going. In the earlier story of the disabled man in John 5, notice how Jesus prompted the man to verbalize his goals by asking him, "Do you want to get well?" There is another healing story in the Bible where Jesus asks a man a similar question. As Jesus and a large crowd of disciples were leaving the city one day, a blind man named Bartimaeus was sitting by the roadside. When he heard that it was Jesus who was passing by, he cried out, "Jesus, Son of David, have mercy on me!" (Mark 10:47). Many in the crowd rebuked him for this, but the Bible says he continued to cry out. Finally, Jesus asked the man, "What do you want me to do for you?" (v. 51). As in the earlier example of the disabled man, this question seems to be out of place. Jesus was used to people coming to him for healing and he knew the man was blind, so why would he ask a blind man what he wants? Perhaps Jesus wants people to verbalize their goals. The blind man responded by saying, "Rabbi, I want to see."

5. *Make your move.* Bartimaeus had heard about the healing miracles of Jesus and now he recognized that Jesus and a large crowd were passing in front of him as he sat by the road. If he were to get Jesus' attention, he must make his move now, but if he hesitates, Jesus will be gone and the opportunity may never come again. I am sure he could imagine all kinds of negative and discouraging statements that could be said about his situation. The crowd was not very sympathetic to his needs, and when he first cried out, many in the crowd rebuked him and told him to be quiet (v. 48). So, Bartimaeus had many reasons not to try and do something about his condition. He had to overcome the inertia of making that first bold move as well as the criticism of the crowd. Besides all of this, what if Jesus actually healed him? All Bartimaeus knew how to do was sit by the road and beg. Although receiving his sight would be wonderful, he would still face the challenges of his changed circumstance once his sight was restored. These were all good reasons for Bartimaeus to hesitate, but if he hesitates, the opportunity for change is gone.

People in the rut of addiction often hesitate when they consider change. Someone said that a rut is like a grave with both ends kicked out, and this description fits those who are stuck in addiction. People can always find reasons why they do not want to change, but initiating change is like starting an exercise program, if you do not make the first move, you will never get started. The following poem illustrates this point:

> I spent a fortune on a trampoline,
> A stationary bike and a rowing machine
> Complete with gadgets to read my pulse,
> And gadgets to prove my progress results,
> And others to show the miles I've charted—
> But they left off the gadget to get me started.

Get Some Flow

I once had a good friend who loved to use the word flow. He was always talking about whether things were flowing properly. Life can also have flow. Flow in life is the positive movement of goals, values, and relationships that occur over time. Positive flow makes life worth living. One of the great benefits of extracurricular activities in school is that they give young people the positive flow that keeps them from destructive behaviors like addiction. Young people who are planning and preparing for their goals and careers in life also have flow, as Peele (2004) says, "Kids who become involved in positive endeavors are less likely to be derailed by drugs, alcohol, or other addictions" (82). But who do we get to talk to teens about drugs and alcohol? We normally get recovering drug addicts whose lives have little or no flow and, as a result, they exaggerate the appeal of drugs. A better strategy is to show young people how important it is to have positive flow in their lives, and that it is in their own best interest to prepare for the future rather than throw their lives away on drugs and alcohol. Positive life flow can offset the appeal of drugs because people recognize they have too much to lose if they choose addiction.

Having flow in life can also determine whether people stop addiction or continue. Granfield and Cloud (1996), who studied natural recovery among drug and alcohol addicts, argue that research shows that those who have a "stake in conventional life" are better able to recover than those who do not (54). If people have no money, job skills, or support network, and if they cannot find things they can value more than their continuing addiction, then it is unlikely they will ever change. When people have something appealing they can return to, they pursue it rather than addiction. What this shows, perhaps, is that the power of addiction is not in the drugs but in the lack of flow in people's lives. If this is the case, then how do you explain the fact that some people pursue addiction despite having positive flow? People choose addiction for a variety of reasons, and the reality that some pursue addiction despite having positive life flow is based on their foolish choices and not their genes or brainwaves. The fact is, fewer people who have flow choose addiction. Of those who do, natural recovery is more likely among those who develop or discover positive flow than those who do not. As an example, consider this respondent's answer to why he stopped his drug addiction, "I'm a father, a husband, and a worker. This is how I see myself today. Being a drug addict was someone I was in the past. I'm over that and I don't think about it anymore" (50).

Positive flow in life helps people acquire the beliefs and values necessary for change. Cognitive therapists tend to view resistance to change as coming from a set of false beliefs, but there is an intermediate step between beliefs and change and that is values. A change in belief must first produce a new set of values. The values produce a change in behavior, as Schaler (1998) notes, "Drug addicts simply have different values from the norm" (246). The difference in values between addicts and non-addicts is significant but seldom accounted for in addiction studies and treatment. Peele (1989) argues "the role of people's value-driven choices is ignored in descriptions of addictions" (146) and the stories of addicts' awakenings are really the establishment or perhaps reawakening of dormant values (188). These values do not have to be religiously based, but they must be strong enough to provide incentive for change.

Maintain the Change

Forming a new identity is difficult, and many people also have difficulty maintaining their new identity, or they go back and forth for a while as they play two roles. Peele (2004) identifies four key areas that are crucial in overcoming an addiction and maintaining change. The areas he cites are relationships, work, leisure activities, and coping skills (102). In addition to these areas, I would add the need to have meaning and purpose in life. Many can find special meaning in relationships, work, and even leisure activities, but an even greater meaning and purpose can be found in biblical religion.

1) Intimacy and family relationships. This includes marriage, family, and children as well as friends. Those who have relationships that are supportive of change are more likely to succeed in staying out of the addiction rut. One benefit of addiction support groups is that they provide an opportunity for those who have burned their bridges with family and friends to find a supportive relationship. Stanton Peele identifies five characteristics in the cultural and family life of people that lead to alcohol and drug addiction, and these characteristics represent a recipe for excess when found in the lives of those who use drugs and alcohol:

1. The individual is not part of a responsible social group and a stable social setting.
2. The individual uses a substance either in isolation or with people who don't or can't care for him or her.
3. The user is introduced to the substance by people whose own use is uncontrolled or harmful.
4. The substance is seen as having magical properties to transform the user, and also as being impossible to control.
5. Use of the substance is seen as an excuse for or signal to engage in antisocial, irresponsible, or uncontrolled behavior. (135)

Notice how these cultural and social characteristics are a significant part of most addicted lifestyles. These characteristics suggest that addiction is a choice because people who gravitate to the opposite of these characteristics either choose not to use drugs and alcohol or, if they do, use drugs and alcohol moderately. Notice also that some people may have positive family and social ties but choose a different cultural and social environment in which to engage in their addictions. The more these characteristics are a part of the social and cultural environments of addicts, the more difficult it is to initiate change.

2) Employment and work. Most people find purpose in their work. Even if people do not like their jobs, they can always view the job as a means to an end; that is, the money they get from the job provides for some significant purpose in their lives. Work that provides money for a worldly focus and short-term gratification is not enough, and work that is viewed as a curse is not healthy or helpful. Work is a blessing and not a curse, and God designed humankind to be involved in some kind of work activity. God put Adam in the Garden of Eden "to work it and take care of it" (Genesis 2:15). The energy, creativity, and ingenuity involved in work is beneficial and provides a healthy distraction from an addiction lifestyle. We are not created to be lazy. Parents who insist that their children work do them a great favor because this sets them on a positive course for their lives. Work skills and accomplishments provide a sense of identity and contribute to positive feelings of self-esteem.

3) Leisure activities. Leisure activities are special interests outside of work that bring pleasure and meaning to life. Sports, fishing, hunting, gardening, cooking, and various hobbies are ways people choose to relax and enjoy themselves outside of work. These activities often bring the necessary flow to life that enables people to focus on things other than addiction.

4) Coping skills. People who experience strong negative feelings over relationship problems and intimacy often turn to addiction because they do not have the necessary coping skills to deal with these issues. They may model the dysfunctional behavior of others in similar circumstances, or they may never have been taught the proper way to handle disappointments. If these skills are lacking, training or therapy can be helpful in providing the necessary coping skills that can provide an alternative to addiction.

5) Meaningful religious involvement. A genuine religious faith and meaningful involvement in church can provide emotional stability and a regular social support group. To begin a new identity, it is helpful to have someone else who has a strong personal identity to act as a guide. One of the purposes of religious association is to provide encouragement to those who are not as strong, "Carry each others burdens, and in this way you will fulfill the law of Christ" (Galatians 6:2). Christian faith also helps people understand the significance of a new identity since this is the kind of language that describes conversion, "Therefore, if anyone is in Christ, he is a new creation; the old has gone, the new has come!" (2 Corinthians 5:17).

6) Flexibility. At times, a new identity requires the use of different strategies to maintain change. If something fails or does not work, we should not try the same thing over and over again. To illustrate, we may have to be flexible about changing our environments, or if our current friends are not supportive of a new identity, we may have to find new friends. If past leisure activities included drinking binges, or activities where drugs and alcohol were consumed, then it is in our own best interest to find new leisure activities.

7) Time. In most cases, it takes a long time for a new identity to fully develop. We need time to process the new perception of ourselves. The length of time may depend on how long the old identity has been a part of our beliefs and how deeply ingrained these beliefs are in our minds. Knowing what to do is half the battle and the longer we spend working on our new identity, the more permanent the change will be. It is likely that our old identity will seek to reassert itself from time to time, but regardless of how long it takes, we must be committed to change.

Conclusion

A major reason that people do not change is a lack of knowledge about their own behaviors. There is nothing mysterious about addiction, and once people conceptualize the significant issues relative to addiction, the easier it is to begin the process toward successful change. Addiction is a behavior, and there are a variety of reasons why people choose to behave in ways that are harmful to themselves and others. Most often, it is due to some faulty belief they have about themselves or their environments, or a failure to understand gratification, or an addiction identity they have adopted. Most addicts choose drug and alcohol addiction as a way to cope with strong feelings, especially feelings relative to broken relationships. Initiating change is difficult because of inertia, or the resistance to making a major course correction in life, but once change has begun, the burden becomes easier to bear the farther one goes in the new direction. A change in beliefs accompanied by a new set of values is the most beneficial way to change behavior. A positive flow in life reinforces and maintains the change.

Recommended Reading

Carlo C. DiClemente (2003) has an excellent book on change titled, *Addiction and Change: How Addictions Develop and Addicted People Recover.* This book will help people conceptualize the path they need to follow in establishing new patterns of behavior. DiClemente emphasizes that the absence of a behavior alone is not sufficient enough to maintain a change, "In order to sustain recovery, new behaviors and reinforcing experiences must become part of a new way of living in the world" (190).

Quantum Change is a book by Miller and C'de Baca (2001) about the major changes that people make when they move away from addiction and toward a more controlled way of living. Not everyone makes a dramatic change like this, but many people change their behavior all at once and never go back to their addiction lifestyles. One value of this book is that if we study change we can better know how to change ourselves.

Questions for Discussions

1. Why is knowing half the battle?
2. Why is it better to allow behavior to determine identity?
3. What are some of the advantages to being a Christian when

it comes to how we identify ourselves? How does Christian conversion relate to the idea of a new identity? What does 2 Corinthians 5:17 teach us about identity?

4. What are the issues surrounding short-term and long-term gratification? Is short-term gratification always bad? Why is this a key concept in addiction?

5. Why are people who have flow better off than people who do not when it comes to addiction? Give some examples of positive life flow.

6. What are some good ways to maintain a change in addiction?

WORKS CITED

Alcoholics Anonymous World Services. (1976). *Alcoholics Anonymous: The Story of How Many Thousands of Men and Women Have Recovered from Alcoholism, (3rd ed.).* New York: Alcoholics Anonymous World Services, Inc.

Alexander, Bruce K., Hadaway, Patricia. & Coambs, Robert. (1980). Rat park chronicle. *British Columbia Medical Journal* 22, no. 2 (February 1980),

_____. & Schweighofer, R. F. (1998). "Defining 'Addiction.'" In Jeffrey A. Schaler, ed. *Drugs: Should we Legalize, Decriminalize or Deregulate?* Amherst, New York: Prometheus Books.

_____. Hadaway, Patricia. & Coambs, Robert. (1998). "Rat Park Chronicle." In Jeffrey A. Schaler, ed. *Drugs: Should we Legalize, Decriminalize or Deregulate?* Amherst, New York: Prometheus Books.

American Psychiatric Association. *Diagnostic and Statistical Manual of Mental Disorders*, Fourth Edition, Text Revision. Washington, DC: American Psychiatric Association, 2000.

Bauer, Walter. (1952). *A Greek-English Lexicon of the New Testament.* Translated by William F. Arndt and F. Wilbur Gingrich. London: The University of Chicago Press.

Beck, Aaron T., Wright, Fred D., Newman, Cory F., & Liese, Bruce S. (1993). *Cognitive Therapy of Substance Abuse.* New York: The Guilford Press.

Breggin, Peter (1991). *Toxic Psychiatry.* New York: St. Martin's Press.

Breggin, Peter (1999). *Your Drug May be Your Problem.* Cambridge, Massachusetts: Perseus Publishing.

Caetano, R. (1987). Public opinions about alcoholism and its treatment. *Journal of Studies on Alcohol*, 48, 153-160.

Ciarrocchi, Joseph W. (2002). *Counseling Problem Gamblers.* New York: Academic Press.

Collins, R. L., Parks, G. & Marlatt, G. A. (1985). Social determinants of alcohol consumption: The effects of social interaction and model status on the self-administration of alcohol. *Journal of Consulting and Clinical Psychology, 53,* 189-200.

Craig, William Lane. (1979). *The Kalam Cosmological Argument.* New York: Barnes & Noble Books.

Erickson, Patricia G. and Alexander, Bruce K. (1998). "Cocaine and Addictive Liability." In Jeffrey A. Schaler, ed., *Drugs: Should we Legalize, Decriminalize or Deregulate?* Amherst, New York: Prometheus Books.

Evans, Katie and Sullivan, J. Michael. (2001). *Dual Diagnosis: Counseling the Mentally Ill Substance Abuser.* New York: The Guilford Press.

Fingarette, Herbert. (1998). "Addiction and Criminal Responsibility." In Jeffrey A. Schaler, ed., *Drugs: Should we Legalize, Decriminalize or Deregulate?* Amherst, New York: Prometheus Books.

Fingarette, Herbert. (1988). *Heavy Drinking.* Berkeley, California: University of California Press.

Fisher, Gary L. & Harrison, Thomas C. (2000). *Substance Abuse: Information for School Counselors, Social Workers, Therapists, and Counselors.* Boston: Allyn and Bacon.

Geisler, Norman. (2001). *Chosen but Free: A Balanced View of Divine Election.* Minneapolis, Minnesota: Bethany House Publishers.

Glasser, William. *Choice Theory* (1998). New York: Harper Collins Publishers.

Glynn, Patrick. (1997). *God, The Evidence.* Rocklin, CA: Prima Publishing.

Granfield, Robert & Cloud, William. (1996). The elephant that no one sees: Natural recovery among middle-class addicts. *Journal of Drug Issues, 26(1),* 45-61.

Grogan, G. W. (1986). *Isaiah.* In The Expositor's Bible Commentary, volume 6. Grand Rapids, Michigan: The Zondervan Corporation.

Hare, Robert D. (1993). *Without Conscience: The Disturbing World of the Psychopaths Among Us.* New York: The Guilford Press.

Heick, Otto W. (1965). *The History of Christian Thought.* Philadelphia: Fortress Press.

Inaba, Darryl S. & Cohen, William E. (2004). *Uppers, Downers, All Arounders: Physical and Mental Effects of Psychoactive Drugs.* CNS Publications, Inc.: Ashland, Oregon.

Jellinek, E. M. (1960). *The Disease Concept of Alcoholism.* New Haven, CT: Hillhouse Press.

Klein, William. (1990). *The New Chosen People: A Corporate View of Election.* Zondervan Publishing House: Grand Rapids, Michigan.

Koenig, Harold G. (2002). The connection between psychoneuroimmunology. In Harold G. Koenig and Harvey Jay Cohen (Eds.), *The Link between Religion and Health: Psychoneuroimmunology and the Faith Factor.* New York: Oxford University Press.

Kurtz, Earnest. (1979). *Not God: A History of Alcoholics Anonymous.* Center City, Minnesota: Hazelden.

Levin, Jeff. (2001). *God, Faith, and Health.* New York: John Wiley & Sons, Inc.

Lindsell, Harold (1976). *The Battle for the Bible.* Grand Rapids, Michigan: Zondervan Publishing House.

Ladouceur, R., Sylvain, C., Boutin, C. & Doucet, C. (1998). *Understanding and Treating the Pathological Gambler.* West Sussex, England: John Wiley and Sons.

Marlatt, G. A. (1983). The controlled-drinking controversy: A commentary. *American Psychologist, 38,* 1097-1110.

——————————. & Gordon, J. R. (1985). *Relapse Prevention: Maintenance Strategies in Addictive Behavior Change.* New York: Guilford.

McMullin, Rian E. (2000). *The New Handbook of Cognitive Therapy Techniques.* New York: W. W. Norton & Company.

——————————. (2005). *Taking Out Your Mental Trash: A Consumer's Guide to Cognitive Restructuring Therapy.* New York: W. W. Norton & Company.

Meichenbaum, Donald. (1985). *Stress Inoculation Training.* Elmsford, NY: Pergamon.

Miller, William R. (1998). Researching the spiritual dimensions of alcohol and other drug problems. *Addiction, 93* (7), 979-991.

Miller, William R. & C'de Baca. (2001). *Quantum Change.* New York: The Guilford Press.

Miller, William R., & Rollnick, Stephen. (2002). *Motivational Interviewing: Preparing People for Change.* New York: The Guilford Press.

Myers, J. B. (2003). *Elders and Deacons: A Biblical Study of Church Leadership.* Nashville, Tennessee: 21st Century Christian.

Peele, Stanton. (1989). *Diseasing of America.* San Francisco: Jossey-Bass Publishers.

_____. (2004). *7 Tools to Beat Addiction.* New York: Three Rivers Press.

Piedmont, R. L. (1999). Does spirituality represent the sixth factor of personality? Spiritual transcendence and the five-factor model. *Journal of Personality, 67,* 985-1013.

Reber, Arthur S. & Reber, Emily. (2001). *The Penguin Dictionary of Psychology.* Third edition. London: Penguin Books.

Rice, John Steadman. (1996). *A Disease of One's Own: Psychotherapy, Addiction, and the Emergence of Co-Dependency.* London: Transaction Publishers.

Robins, Lee N., Helzer, John E., Hesselbrock, Michi, & Wish, Eric. (1998). Vietnam Veterans Three Years after Vietnam: How our study Changed Our View of Heroin." In Jeffrey A. Schaler, ed. *Drugs: Should we Legalize, Decriminalize or Deregulate?* Amherst, New York: Prometheus Books.

Schaler, Jeffrey A. (1996). Spiritual thinking in addiction treatment providers: The Spiritual Belief Scale (SBS). *Alcohol Treatment Quarterly, 14,* 7-33.

_____. (1998). "Drugs and Free Will." In Jeffrey A. Schaler, ed., *Drugs: Should we Legalize, Decriminalize or Deregulate?* Amherst, New York: Prometheus Books.

_____. (2000). *Addiction is a Choice.* Chicago: Open Court.

Seligman, Martin E. P. (1998). *Learned Optimism: How to Change Your Mind and Your Life.* New York: Pocket Books.

_____. (2002). *Authentic Happiness.* New York: The Free Press.

_____. (1993). *What You Can Change...And What You Can't.* New York: Ballantine Books.

Sobell, Mark B. & Sobell Linda C. (1993). *Problem drinkers: Guided Self-Change Treatment.* New York: The Guilford Press.

Spiegel D. & Fawzy I. (2002). Psychosocial interventions and prognosis in cancer. In Harold G. Koenig and Harvey Jay Cohen (Eds.), *The Link between Religion and Health: Psychoneuroimmunology and the Faith Factor.* New York: Oxford University Press.

The National Council on Alcoholism and Drug Dependence. (1990). Definition of alcoholism. Retrieved August 1, 2006 from http://www.ncadd.org/facts/defalc.html.

Thomas, Robert L. (1978). *1 Thessalonians*. In The Expositor's Bible Commentary, volume 11. Grand Rapids, Michigan: The Zondervan Corporation.

Toneatto, T., Blitz-Miller, T., Calderwood, K., Dragonetti, R., & Tsanos, A. (1997). Cognitive distortions in heavy gambling. *Journal of Gambling Studies, 13*, 253-266.

Vaillant, George. (1983). *The Natural History of Alcoholism*. London: Harvard University Press.

Valverde, Mariana. (1998). *Diseases of the Will*. New York: Cambridge University Press.

White, William L. (1998). *Slaying the Dragon*. Bloomington, Illinois: Lighthouse Institute.

Williams, Redford B. (2002). Hostility, neuroendocrine changes, and health outcomes. In Harold G. Koenig and Harvey Jay Cohen (Eds.), *The Link between Religion and Health: Psychoneuroimmunology and the Faith Factor*. New York: Oxford University Press.

1158949